The Little Earth Book

James Bruges

To James' children: Ben, Clare, Kate and Bea
and to Alastair's children: Toby and Rowan

fragile earth an imprint of **Alastair Sawday Publishing**

4th Edition

Written and researched by James Bruges
Published by Alastair Sawday Publishing
Editors: Alastair Sawday and Rachel Fielding
Production Manager: Julia Richardson
Cover design: Caroline King
Overall design concept: Caroline King
Page layout: Paul Groom
Original illustrations: Mark Brierley
and David Atkinson
Cover image: ©ImageState
Printing: Pims Print, Yeovil

Fourth edition (updated and revised) 2004
Copyright © 2000, 2001, 2002, 2004
Alastair Sawday Publishing Co. Ltd

Published by Alastair Sawday Publishing Co. Ltd
The Home Farm, Barrow Gurney, Bristol BS48 3RW

Published in the USA by The Disinformation Company Ltd
163 Third Avenue, Suite 108 New York, NY 10003

A catalogue record for this book is available from the
British Library.

ISBN 1-901970-52-3

Contents

4

5

Introduction

Photographs from space show the world shrouded in a thin veil of atmosphere. This gaseous film is the reason why there is life on our planet and not on others; without it the earth would be frozen, pitted and dead. Like Mars.

It took over two billion years for living cells to transform the toxic soup of the atmosphere. Oxygen combined with other elements to foster the rich variety of life that we know today. Gases interacted with bacteria, plankton and plants. Carbon was captured by photosynthesis and laid down in the earth's crust as coal, oil and gas. Complex systems of biodiversity evolved partly with complementary synergy, partly as a balance of competing interests and partly by the erection of barriers between species – all life forms interacting in ways that we will never fully comprehend. Humanity inherited a magical domain, a fascinating, beautiful and healthy world at a comfortable temperature.

But we are digging up much that was laid down, and disgorging it back onto the earth's crust and into the atmosphere. We are felling the planet's lungs, the ancient forests. We are causing mass extinctions and reducing biodiversity. We are unsettling the evolved balance of life by creating novel chemicals, gases, bacteria, viruses, plants and animals that have never been part of nature's evolutionary processes, and allowing them to spread over the earth's surface. We are causing global warming on a scale not seen since the end of the Permian period when carbon dioxide emissions from volcanoes started a chain of events that destroyed nearly all life. Earth is running backwards into the sterile toxic chaos from which it evolved.

Over 1,600 scientists, including four-fifths of all Nobel science prizewinners, issued the famous World Scientists' Warning to Humanity in 1992. It included these comments: "We are fast approaching many of the Earth's limits. Current economic practices that damage the environment cannot continue. Our massive tampering could trigger unpredictable collapse of critical biological systems that are only partly understood. A great change in our stewardship of the Earth and the life on it is required if vast human misery is to be avoided and our global home on this planet is not to be irretrievably mutilated." In the ensuing decade we have not changed course. Already a third of the planet's 'natural wealth' has been lost. Human misery on an unprecedented scale may result from the headlong rush of the wealthy for global exploitation. We may be guilty of the ultimate crime against humanity – allowing the earth's support systems to crumble while we enjoy the temporary benefits of an unsustainable lifestyle.

And human society is crumbling. The atrocities of the 11th September against the World Trade Center and the Pentagon – symbols of corporate capitalism and military dominance – raised a question mark over the West's breathtaking project to bring all cultures throughout the world into a single economic and trade empire in which people, everywhere, are defined not by their culture but as consumers, customers and competitors. Society's essential services are being wrested from governments and handed to corporations whose motivation is profit. The global economy is precarious and growth, though impossible on a finite planet, is offered as the only prescription. Civil society is in conflict with institutions that put the rights of money above the rights of society. The policies of these global institutions have failed – the world is littered with collapsed and collapsing states, inequality has risen to obscene levels and commodity prices, on which the poor depend for income, have been driven down remorselessly so that half the world now lives on less than $2 a day. Anger against the West has exploded in Central and South America, the Middle East, Africa and Asia. Asymmetric warfare, with ultra-sophisticated hardware on one side and terror on the other, could bring unprecedented destruction. Our civilisation has taken a wrong turning – but we can choose a different path.

There are inspiring examples of people thinking, acting and dreaming concepts for a new direction. Knowledge is not the whole answer – we exploit what we know but defend what we love. The atmosphere is now appreciated as a global common so that equal carbon-emission rights, within a sustainable total, would give a basic income to everyone in addition to providing the incentive for all people and countries to reduce emissions. The monetary system could be re-designed to keep us within the earth's carrying capacity, to be stable, encourage local market exchange and end currency gambling. Technologies such as hydrogen fuel cells and biomimicry could reduce damage. Trade could operate cooperatively. Poor countries could be encouraged and helped to nurture their infant industries thus adding value within their borders and finding their own solutions to poverty that are not dependent on charity. Our genetic knowledge could strengthen an organic agriculture that is in harmony with earth's systems, supports rural communities and gives security to productive small farmers. Local participation, local economies and local democracy could reverse the alienation that is crippling society. We could revisit the unique constitution of the United States and the ideals of its Founders who struggled against corporate tyranny and resolved that government of the people, by the people, and for the people shall not perish from the earth.

But change must be radical. These proposals are realistic, not utopian. If the scale of remedial action fails to match the scale of the crises, we face catastrophe.

How to use this book

> *"A single tiny island (England) is today keeping the world in chains.*
> *If an entire nation of 300 million took to similar economic*
> *exploitation it would strip the world bare like locusts."*
> Mohandas Gandhi, 1928

Dip in and out as you wish. Take one part at a time. Each chapter is short and to the point, however vast the subject, and aims to provoke you both emotionally and intellectually whether or not you agree with everything said. Many chapters refer you to books though the views expressed here do not necessarily represent the views of those books.

Better still, try reading it all at one or two sittings so that the ideas, held together in your memory, will form an interconnected whole. These global issues must not be viewed in isolation. Our attitude to the environment, trade, militarism, genetics, as well as our underlying philosophy, act on each other. Please do not skip the chapters on economics, hardly the most seductive of subjects, because faulty economics is at the root of most of our problems and, actually, the reasons are not difficult to understand.

Think how you might influence your representatives. We cannot predict the future with any accuracy but each step can be either towards or away from environmental survival and social justice. We do not have to submit to the faulty dictates of political cliques of whichever party – another world is possible. Also think of ways in which your own life and that of your community could make a difference. As Adlai Stephenson said of Eleanor Roosevelt: **"She would rather light candles than curse the darkness, and her glow has warmed the world."**

"History is a race between education and catastrophe."
H.G. Wells

Cod

a symbol for our times

"After you, sir..."

The best fishing grounds in the world were off the coast of New England and the prize fish were cod. On Cabot's return from there in 1497 it was reported "the sea is swarming with fish which can be taken not only with the net but in baskets let down with a stone." A hundred years later cod were reported as big as a man and the fishing grounds served the whole of Europe.

Cod swim in large shoals just above the seabed. They have a long life cycle, spawning only when, after four years, they are large enough. When trawl nets were introduced they scooped up all the fish, big and small, and few lasted long enough to spawn.

It was not until the 1980s that the coastal fishermen of New England realised that, thanks to big offshore trawlers, the cod were disappearing, but the US government took no action. So by 1992 the cod were gone. With the fish went the fishermen. Their skills in navigation, gutting, net mending and fish marketing didn't help them. They were also a unique species that will be hard to replace. The tourists who enjoy the picturesque sailing ships in Gloucester harbour are now served filleted cod from Russia and fishermen cut the hotel lawns.

Fishermen will now have to wait up to 15 years for the stocks of cod to return, if they ever do. Young cod are no longer migrating to warmer waters to spawn, perhaps because there are no older cod to lead them. Arctic cod, which have no market value, are moving in and they eat Atlantic cod eggs and larvae. Other species and predators are upsetting the natural balance and may also prevent rejuvenation of cod stocks. So the most prolific fishing grounds in the world may now be dead.

It is a different story in Norway where there was a crisis in the 1980s. Fish stocks were seriously depleted, catches were falling. The government took drastic action that put many fishermen and boat builders out of work, but within three years stocks improved and the fishing trade was saved.

Sixty percent of the world's ocean fisheries are now at or near the point at which yields decline, yet governments still provide massive subsidies to their fishing fleets. An international quota system has been introduced but even that has perverse effects: a third of the fish caught are thrown back dead, and only the higher value catch retained.

But the story gets worse. Warmer water is depleting some species. Chemicals from rivers cause plankton blooms that deprive fish of oxygen. Fish farming is a partial solution but it has severe problems too: interbreeding passes defective genes to wild fish, the farms act as hothouses for disease, farmed salmon are found to contain PCB gender-benders, intensively used antibiotics and pesticides pollute coastal waters. The farms need a lot of fish-food - it takes 10 kg

of trawled wild fish (yes, it's made into fish food) from countries like Peru to feed 2 kg of farmed Atlantic salmon; thus Peruvian coastal fishermen are deprived of their staple diet and livelihood - to serve the sophisticated tastes of the rich.

Freshwater species have also declined globally. The 1995 catch was 45% lower than that of 1970. Shrimp farms in East Asia are rarely productive for more than five to ten years, after which the land is unusable due to severe pollution; this temporary industry produces cheap shrimps and undercuts the sustainable production of traditional shrimp farmers.

It may be possible to start restoring the life of the oceans if billions of dollars are not given in subsidies for over fishing, if the certification of seafood from well-managed sources is promoted, if coral reefs are effectively protected, if chemical flows from fields to rivers to oceans are checked, if a network of protected marine areas is enforced, if a moratorium is imposed on unregulated fishing in marine ecosystem hot spots and if local communities are given power over their fisheries.

St Lucia's corals were damaged and the reefs over-fished. Now half the corals have been put out of bounds. The fish are back because they have somewhere to breed and tourists still have corals to enjoy.

Fish provide just one example of a faulty theory. Somehow market fundamentalism, a belief that free unfettered trade will resolve all problems, has captured the imagination of politicians and flat-earth economists. While fish were plentiful it may have made some sense. When stocks decline it is fish, not money or markets, that matter – the same is true of all other primary products.

It only takes a moment's thought with fish in mind to realise that **market fundamentalism is a remarkably silly idea**. Cod were once a symbol of hope; they are now a warning to the world.

The North Sea having been irretrievably harmed, it has taken only twelve years for some deep sea stocks off the West coast of Britain to be driven close to extinction. Some of these become sexually mature only after 30 years so will not recover.

West African fisheries are on the brink of collapse due to over fishing by the European Union. No one asked the native fishermen if they minded losing their livelihood.

The world's fishing industry produces $70 billion worth of fish. It receives $54 billion in subsidies.

Only 10% of Caribbean coral reefs are intact.

Declining cod catch in the North Sea

30 Cod

Cod
Mark Kurlansky 1999

Don't Predict!

just be systematic

"Heavier-than-air flying machines are impossible", declared the eminent physicist Lord Kelvin in 1895. The chairman of IBM was wrong too: "I think there is a world market for maybe five computers", said Thomas Watson in 1943. Then scientists predicted that nuclear electricity would be too cheap to meter, and that oil would become scarce by the 1990s; we now extract more than ever. Anyway, we like to think that something will replace oil if it does run out, so why not carry on using it as before? Predictions and their failures can both be misleading.

Instead of guessing at the future we should think systematically about the past and the present – about things we actually know – and **we must live within the rules set by nature.** In a world of finite resource, what is used today will be denied our children – which simple logic avoids the uncertainty of when it might run out. To base our whole economy on gobbling up non-renewable resources like oil, phosphorus and aquifer water is obviously stupid. There are four principles of sustainability that need to be respected, systematically:

♦ All the toxic minerals like mercury or fossil resources that we dig out of the earth, refine and use will eventually degrade back into the land, water and air and cause cumulative pollution. **We must not extract more than can be permanently contained or safely re-absorbed.**

♠ We live in a balanced ecology that evolved over a period of four billion years. When we introduce new stable molecules, bacteria, viruses, plants, creatures and radioactivity that disturb this balance, they will cause problems somewhere, sometime. **We must not allow these products of society to increase in nature.**

♣ The world's flora, moisture and biodiversity form interconnected natural cycles that support life and a stable atmosphere. **We must not diminish this life-support system.**

♥ The fourth principle concerns equity. The poor, the majority of the world's population, will not endure a distribution of resources that is manifestly unfair. **We must recognise that all people in the world have an equal right to the benefits of nature.**

We must test each human activity systematically and reject it if it offends any of the above principles. There is nothing woolly about sustainability; it is hard-edged, uncompromising, quantifiable and scientifically rigorous. The rules are set by nature, not by man.

The financial world is similar. Commentators constantly predicted that the Dow Jones Index would continue to rise, and they still do. It tumbled but, in the future – who knows? Predictions can be self-fulfilling. The very act of participating in markets influences those markets. The world hung on the words of Alan Greenspan, chairman of the Federal Reserve. If he wanted he could have brought the whole pack of cards tumbling down by making a rash prediction; no wonder his face is so heavily lined. Yet he preferred to remain inscrutable – "if I seem unduly clear to you" he once told a congressman "you must have misunderstood what I said."

Every businessman and gambler would love to predict the future accurately, and every day the financial pages try to help him or her. But the most superficial look at the financial system indicates that it is inherently unjust, unstable and as predictable as the weather. We leave it to the experts who have a vested interest in keeping it inscrutable. The best we can do is keep our fingers crossed in the hope that we may strike lucky.

The economy, like our environmental intervention, has grown exponentially and no one can predict where this will lead. But it should be obvious that we will be in deep trouble if we cannot re-model it to protect the ecosystem and to move, systematically, towards equity and stability.

The Natural Step
Karl-Hendrik Robert 2002

Ozone Layer

a ray of hope

If there were no ozone in the stratosphere there would be little life on earth.

Ozone is a gas, a form of oxygen. It is dispersed in a 20-mile layer of the upper atmosphere where it shields us from ultraviolet (UV) radiation. It is so dilute that if it were all brought down to sea level it would be no thicker than a china plate. Until the ozone layer was in place, nearly two billion years ago, life was limited to primitive forms of algae in the oceans.

In the 1970s scientists worried that within 50 years the ozone layer might reduce by three percent. By the late 1980s this had already happened. But, even worse, by 1996 a hole larger than the US had developed over the Antarctic, another hole was growing over the Arctic, and there was a 20% reduction over much of the world.

UV-B has had a lot of publicity because it causes skin cancers. But it also reduces resistance to AIDS, tuberculosis and herpes, causes cataracts and blindness, reduces the growth and yield of most food crops and kills plankton in the sea (affecting the fish population and also reducing plankton's pivotal role in extracting carbon dioxide from the air). With increased exposure to UV-B the genes in some plants relocate in the genome causing mutations and disrupting the plant's development and fertility. Changes to the DNA of plants and animals could permeate the food chain. Ozone holes are seriously bad news!

How is the ozone layer destroyed?

The major culprits are chlorofluoro-carbon (CFCs), though halide and bromine containing substances, widely used in pesticides, are also responsible. CFCs are artificial chemicals that have been widely used in propellants, refrigerants, insulation, cleaning agents and packaging. They are non-toxic, have no smell and are non-flammable, so for 40 years were considered benign. There seemed to be no reason to restrict their use. But they offend a fundamental law of sustainability being stable gases not found in nature and somehow, sometime, they were bound to cause problems. We can now only regret that legislators did not invoke the precautionary principle earlier.

When CFC molecules are exposed to strong UV radiation in the upper atmosphere they are broken up and release chlorine atoms that attack the ozone. A single chlorine atom can destroy many thousands of ozone molecules. If CFC emissions were stopped today the chemical reactions would continue for decades. Other processes contribute to ozone damage: the destruction of tropical forests, increases in cattle ranching, cattle-feed with a high protein content, artificial fertilisation of rice, the use of chemicals like the methyl bromide in pesticides.

There are, however, signs of hope. In 1987, the Montreal Protocol required industrial countries to halt CFC production and it banned trading in products containing CFCs.

The protocol was based on the precautionary principle before all scientists agreed that there was a problem. Although the protocol calls for a global ban by 2006 many industries, particularly in the US, have acted early.

But there are still problems. Russia's economic crisis slowed its programme and a black-market in CFCs developed. A refrigerator in every home in China will massively increase its use of CFC. And, if the present US administration bows to industry pressure and exempts methyl bromide from the Protocol, the agreement could be blown apart – destroying the only grounds for hope that humanity can save itself. But if these dangers are avoided the ozone layer could be back to normal in 50 years, demonstrating that humanity is capable of rational cooperation.

In 2002 there was great optimism because the Antarctic ozone hole had shrunk. But in the 2003 it was back, larger than ever.

Protecting the Ozone Layer
Andersen & Sarma

Water

fresh water is running out

Rain is our only sustainable source of fresh water. We ignore this simple fact at our peril.

Fly over the prairie states of America and you will see clusters of dark circles like tiny coins in a desert landscape. Actually, each circle is cultivation, half a mile in diameter, irrigated from a single drop-well and rotating arm. Previously the land had thin grass and wandering herds of buffalo. Now it produces wheat with a higher yield than anywhere in the world. The grain exports from this area are vital for financing America's imports and are a major contributor to feeding the growing world population. It is a miracle of modern agriculture.

Underneath lies the biggest aquifer in the world. Water from melting glaciers seeped into gravel at the end of the last ice age and has been there ever since. It was found in the 1920s and its extraction really got under way in the 1960s. Four to six feet of water is now extracted each year and nature puts back only half an inch. It could last five years or it could last 30 years. No one knows. Farmers believed that this breadbasket was so valuable that the government would provide a massive water project to meet their needs if it ever ran out, like diverting the Mississippi. So they did nothing to economise on the use of water. The future is more likely to be a return of the Dust Bowl that devastated the area in the 1930s.

Most freshwater in the world is in aquifers but getting water from them is sometimes dangerous. All over the world the aquifers are being depleted. Some are finite reservoirs that will never be replaced. Some are replenished from surface water but even these have problems. 60% of the nitrate fertiliser we apply when farming remains in the soil and gradually seeps into the groundwater where it is joined by such pollutants as sewage from leaking pipes and chemicals from rusty fuel tanks. Already a major aquifer in China has serious problems with nitrates and some in Britain are laced with benzene. The US and some other countries have increasing arsenic pollution.

Irrigation requires organisation, so brought the first civilisations into existence. But salt may have destroyed them.

With irrigation, if there is an impervious substrate the water does not drain and salts are drawn to the roots of plants. If the land is drained, however, the salt accumulates in rivers, and evaporation from dam reservoirs concentrates the saltiness. By 1973 the salinity of the Colorado River, where it crossed the border into Mexico's most fertile region, was liquid death to plants.

Water is more valuable than gold – as King Midas found, you can't drink gold. We are as dependent on water to drink as we are on air to breathe but we know even less about groundwater than we know about the weather. How much pollution is already in the ground? How long will it take to get into aquifers? How fast will it spread? How can we extract the pollution? The cost of purifying water is escalating though this is not charged to the polluters – the farmers, the oil companies and the sewerage system. "Let them drink bottled water" will be the cry when it becomes too expensive to provide clean tap water. And the poor will only get drinking water if they can pay for it.

Dams are the other source of irrigation. It is strange that the US followed the communist policy of providing virtually free water to its farmers from federal-funded dams, thus encouraging waste – just as in Russia. There was an orgy of construction before dam building finally stopped in the early 1980s. Virtually all US rivers now have dams. There are 80,000: 50,000 are significant, 2,000 are among the biggest construction projects in the world. But the dams have a finite life as they gradually fill with silt.

Already dams are being dismantled. The US is now casting envious eyes on Canada's abundant free-flowing rivers and, when the US gets desperate, its neighbours have much to fear. Do the Canadians want to lose their beautiful valleys, their salmon and their white-water rafting? Under NAFTA free trade rules Canada may not be able to protect its heritage.

Dams have also seduced India, replacing and destroying centuries-old methods of water-harvesting using bunds, channels and *tank*a. The Sardar Sarovar dam, at present under construction in earthquake-prone Gujarat on a silt-laden river, has a massive 290-mile concrete irrigation canal that will not be filled for 20 years but is already cracking. Upstream, the Bargi dam, completed in 1990, irrigates only 8,000 hectares but flooded 27,000 hectares of fertile land and displaced 115,000 people into city slums. Lessons were not learnt.

Global consumption of freshwater is doubling every 20 years. At present:
- 10% is used by people
- 65% is used by industrial agriculture
- 25% is used by industry.

Ancient Civilisations

In 2,400 BC, irrigated fields in Sumeria produced 2,500 litres of barley per hectare, a respectable yield even by modern standards. By 1,700 BC the yield fell to 900 litres per hectare. Soon afterwards, crop failures began – and that was the end of Sumeria. Most of the great civilisations that depended on irrigation went the same way – salts came to the surface and destroyed their agriculture.

But Egypt, fertile since the Pharaohs, was an exception. Each year the Nile floods the fields, deposits rich new silt and flushes the surface salts out to sea. Well, it did until 1970 when the Aswan high dam was built. The silt no longer renews the land each year, salts are no longer washed away and the delta fishery is declining fast. What's more, the reservoir behind the dam is rapidly filling with the silt that should be fertilizing the fields below.

Cadillac Desert
Mark Reisner 1993

Ecological Footprints

the rich wear big boots

Kerala is beautiful. Canals shaded by coconut palms, markets beside the water, kids playing on the banks. Walk the streets of Trichur and you catch laughing eyes as groups chat and women display their colourful saris. There are plenty of festivals. Then return home and you are struck by how drab and glum everyone looks.

India
Available
America

Kerala is one of the poorest states in India. Yet the infant mortality rate in Kerala is lower than in some European countries, life expectancy is 72 years (higher than that of black people in the US), 95% of Keralans over the age of seven can read and write, it has a higher proportion of its population with postgraduate degrees than the US, 82% of families own their own homes and all have three meals a day. The Hindu half of the population has been matriarchal – where daughters inherit property equally. Importantly, the population is stable and the low birth rate is credited to the high level of female literacy.

What has all this to do with ecological footprints? An 'ecological footprint' is the productive land needed to support people in their lifestyle. An American gets his food, minerals and oil from all over the world and all these things use the world's limited productive land. His 'footprint' is at least 30 times larger than an Indian's. The world has 1.5 hectares of productive land available for each person but, to support present consumption, the world needs 2.3 hectares per person. We are already exceeding limits. This excessive human footprint is trampling productive land so our resource base is decreasing:

10% of land on which food is grown was lost in the last 30 years.

 forest, freshwater and marine environments have reduced by 30% in 30 years.

 a third of all fish species and a quarter of all mammal species are in danger of extinction.

So while the population is increasing the world's resources are decreasing at an alarming rate, and **if everyone adopted the western lifestyle we would need four earths to support us.** But, as Mark Twain commented, "The problem with land is they stopped making it some time ago."

China has developed a taste for western-style consumerism and plans to expand its economy four-fold in the next 20 years. Its people are encouraged to eat an egg every other day for health and the 1.3 billion chickens will need as much grain as Australia produces. For three extra beers a year it will need all of Norway's grain. If the Chinese develop Japan's taste for fish they will consume the world's entire catch. The number of cars in China rose 40% in 2002 and its main manufacturer aims to increase output fivefold in the next few years, but there is simply not enough steel or oil in the world for China to match western car use. The United States uses a third of the world's natural resources but China has already overtaken it as the leading consumer of meat, fertiliser, steel and coal.

Back to Kerala. They are not harming the earth; their education, health and longevity are comparable with those of the west; their women have equality; their population is stable. They show that one can have a satisfactory lifestyle with a footprint that is well within the carrying capacity of the world – i.e. sustainable. Perhaps we should be looking at their culture for lessons in how to create a sustainable culture for ourselves.

When Gandhi was asked for his views on western civilisation he replied: "I think it would be a good idea."

20% of the global population in rich countries consume 86% of the world's resources.

It is now predicted that the Amazon could become a desert like the Sahara.

Plan B
Lester R Brown 2003

An Oxymoron?

sustainable development

In Bali fruit fell from trees and life revolved around music and festival. In Ladakh culture flourished in an extreme climate. In Kenya the Maasai lived in harmony with migrating herds, probably showing continuity from the very origin of our species – Abel, beloved of God, till slain by Cain, the modern farmer and park ranger. China discovered most of our inventions but chose not to use them. The word 'idiot' originated in Greece to describe anyone who did not spend much of his time in public debate. Islam showed how a classless society was possible, developed philosophy and built the most engagingly beautiful buildings like the Taj and the Alhambra. Cultures grew in response to regional conditions, and excess time and wealth were used for buildings, art, ceremonies and jewellery. For four thousand years of civilisation consumption hardly increased but **we are left with evidence of wonderful cultural richness.**

Then on 20 January 1949, in his inauguration speech, President Truman defined most of the world as 'underdeveloped areas' where 'greater production is the key to prosperity and peace'. Set against this was Gandhi's previous warning in 1908 "should India ever resolve to imitate England" he said "it would be the ruin of the nation." Gandhi lost and Truman won.

The majority-nations took up the idea of 'development' with enthusiasm. Rich countries cut slices from their cake-of-wealth to feed the poor, but they still believed that the magic cake would grow forever and the rich would never need to reduce its own portion. In the end everyone would be satisfied.

Within a few years it became apparent that development was not producing jobs, so 'manpower development' became the theme.

Then after 10 years it was realised that hardship persisted so 'social development' was the key phrase at conferences, followed by the 'basic needs approach' and 'equitable development'. The one thing that could never be questioned was the concept of development itself.

Eventually it was realised that the magic cake was not growing and might even be shrinking. So 'sustainable development' was introduced. There is now an army of ecocrats drawing up papers and attending conferences, busily working out how to do more with less. Light bulbs become more efficient. Cars are shared and oil companies plant trees to absorb their fumes. Cities find all sorts of ways to call themselves sustainable. The ecocrats struggle to bring appropriate technology, 'forgiveness' and justice to the poor. Even nature itself has been renamed 'natural capital' so that it can be included in the sums. It is all very comforting.

The driving force behind sustainable development is the no pain theory, the promise that we can achieve social justice without changing in any ways that might be uncomfortable – or is it just putting off the unpalatable moment of truth when we realise that development has been only on behalf of, and to salve the conscience of, the rich. After 55 years of development over half the world is still desperately poor.

> Perhaps four thousand years of culture were rather more nourishing than fifty years of development.

Politicians love grand development gestures. In India they propose to link all the major rivers with canals. The scheme is so expensive it could only be carried out with private capital thus handing India's entire water resource to corporations. And it could be an ecological disaster. Local water-harvesting methods would be more effective at a fraction of the cost – almost all parts of the subcontinent have adequate rain if it is properly managed.

Development can be wiped out by human-induced global warming. Following Hurricane Mitch in 1998 the Honduran president commented, "We lost in 72 hours what we have taken more than fifty years to build."

Atmospheric Carbon

the ultimate weapon of mass destruction

Two hundred million years ago, when planet earth was recovering from extinctions at the end of Permian period, forests covered the land, the atmosphere held a lot of carbon dioxide, the air was warmer than now and the oceans were 200 feet higher. Gradually algae, bacteria, plankton and plants, through photosynthesis, captured carbon from the air and released oxygen. As the plants decayed, coal, gas and oil were laid down in the crust of the earth. The concentration of greenhouse gases reduced, the earth cooled and water levels fell. But the process has been put in reverse for the last 200 years.

Scientists have known about this for a long time. The influence on climate of various gases in the atmosphere was first identified in 1827 by Joseph Fourier, a French mathematician. John Tyndall, an Irish scientist, took on the idea. Then in 1898 Arrhenius, a Swedish scientist, coined the phrase 'greenhouse effect' and predicted that if concentrations of carbon dioxide in the atmosphere doubled the global climate would warm by 4-6°C, figures remarkably close to current predictions. Scientists continued to argue for a hundred more years but the connection between human-induced emission of greenhouse gases and climate-change is now universally accepted, except by a few oil industry oddballs.

Greenhouse gases blanket the earth and without them it would be 30°C colder, frozen and lifeless. Water vapour accounts for 60 percent of the effect but it changes state as gas, cloud or water. Carbon dioxide accounts for over a quarter. We are in an interglacial period during which, for the last 10,000 years, average global temperatures have been around 15°C, making it possible for humans to cultivate land and build civilisations. Carbon dioxide content during interglacials was higher than normal but never rose above 300 ppmv (parts per million by volume).

uncharted territory

carbon dioxide concentrations
during the last 400,000 years
(showing interglacial periods)
and current predictions
(Vostok ice core data)

predicted concentrations
under present policies,
including introduction of
renewables and greater
energy-efficiency:
700 ppmv by 2,100
and rising to 2,000 ppmv

predicted concentrations
if carbon dioxide emissions
are reduced by 70% globally
550 ppmv
(= 40 million years ago)

present concentrations
370 ppmv
(= 3 million years ago)

2 —
0 —
- 2 —
- 4 —
- 6 —
- 8 —
local temperature at Vostok, degrees C

ice-age

settled
agriculture

300

200

100
parts per million by volume

400,000 years ago

300,000 years ago

200,000 years ago

100,000 years ago

1,000 AD

1,500 AD

2,000 AD

Carbon dioxide concentrations started to rise with the Industrial Revolution when we began to mine and burn coal, releasing the trapped carbon back into the atmosphere. The extraction of oil, which started about 100 years ago, released more carbon. Early last century the concentration of carbon dioxide exceeded the highest levels ever experienced in the 400,000 years for which accurate measurements are available. In the last 50 years concentrations have been increasing even faster, passing 370 ppmv. Even if drastic measures are now taken they will continue to rise to at least 500 ppmv. We have entered uncharted territory. Global warming has only just started and we may be too late to stop it. How much will global temperatures change? How high will sea levels rise? **We are facing a global emergency on a scale never experienced before.**

Scientists have sophisticated computer models based on what is known. Cosmic rays affect the clouds. Our distance from the sun varies on a 100,000-year cycle, the earth tilts over a period of 40,000 years, it wobbles over a period of 23,000 years and the sun's intensity varies. These periods are so long they may be of only academic interest. 'Positive feedback effects' could be more immediate. The area of snow is reducing. Snow is white and reflects heat but when snow melts, dark ground or water is exposed and absorbs heat, causing more warming – so more melting – so more dark surfaces – more warming – more melting. This particular positive feedback effect presents a huge danger. But Hadley Centre models show that forests, ground surfaces and the oceans, the natural sinks that absorb CO_2 at present, may each reverse with global warming and result in more positive feedback effects.

Methane and carbon dioxide, twice the amount contained in all fossil fuels, are trapped in gas hydrates under arctic ice and tundra. If only a part is released warming might get out of control – polar temperatures are rising five times as fast as general warming and there are widespread reports of tundra melting. Might this cause runaway global warming? The methane threat has not been fed into current computer models. Methane is a greenhouse gas 20 times more effective than carbon dioxide and scientists used to think it was the real problem. They may have been right. When the Intergovernmental Panel on Climate Change (IPCC) was advising the Rio Summit in 1992, a poll of its scientists found that 51 of the 113 questioned believed that runaway global warming was a possibility. Fifteen of these scientists believed it 'probable'. A Martian would be bewildered by our inaction: "are the rulers of this planet mad, bad or just totally incompetent?"

Beware of predictions. The IPCC initially predicted a temperature rise of 3°C but a few years later doubled the figure. In June 2003 scientists raised the prediction to 10°C due to the effect of small particles. They are constantly reported as being 'surprised' by incidents. In early 2002, for instance, scientists were 'astonished' at the collapse of the 1,250-square-mile Antarctic Larsen B ice shelf in just one month. Perhaps the most sensible comment came from Vladimir Shatalov, a cosmonaut who had the experience of passing through the greenhouse blanket: **"Beyond air there is only emptiness, coldness and darkness. The boundless blue sky, which gives us breath and protects us from the endless black and death, is but an infinitesimally thin film. How dangerous it is to threaten even the smallest part of this gossamer, this conserver of life."**

Runaway warming has happened before. There is only one natural system that matches our ability to release carbon back into the atmosphere – volcanoes. There have been some spectacular eruptions but, to match human emissions, you have to go right back to the end of the Permian period. 250 million years ago eruptions in Siberia emitted carbon dioxide that raised global temperatures 6°C, roughly what is predicted as a result of our current emissions. The consequent melting of polar ice and tundra released gas hydrates to cause runaway warming. Almost all life on earth was extinguished and, without plant roots holding it in place, most of the soil was washed into oceans. Evolution stalled for ten million years while planet earth recovered.

But that was ages ago so could it possibly be a relevant warning for today? Hopefully not. But scientists like to have evidence and there is no evidence to suggest a different outcome.

The Last Hours of Ancient Sunlight
Thom Hartmann 1999

Ostrich Policy

dealing with uncertainty

> If half a degree of global warming is causing hurricanes, cyclones and floods, what will 6 degrees do?

In 2002 the National Academy of Sciences (NAS), the leading US scientific body, gave an even more alarming assessment than the IPCC.

The NAS said that climate changes happen abruptly, not evenly over long periods of time as previously thought but within a few years, maybe a decade or two. Its report says "an abrupt climate change occurs when the climate system is forced to cross some threshold, triggering a new state at a rate determined by the climate system itself and faster than the cause." It illustrated this with the diagram of a seesaw, where a slight shift of weight over the pivot causes the whole structure to tip. The NAS report concludes, "On the basis of the inference from the paleoclimatic record, it is possible that **the projected change will occur not through gradual evolution, proportional to greenhouse gas concentrations, but through abrupt and persistent regime shifts** affecting sub continental or larger regions."

Forget about what might happen to our grandchildren. The climatic seesaw might tip anytime now.

And there is another issue. The sun has increased in luminosity by 30% since life on earth began but the temperature and conditions on earth have remained relatively stable. This remarkable phenomenon gave rise to the Gaia hypothesis that organisms regulate the environment to maintain a temperature that is suitable for life. This might suggest that stability will be maintained whatever we do. James Lovelock, the originator of the science, gives no comfort. He does not consider that the present period is stable. "An interglacial like now," he says "is a period when regulation has temporarily failed and is certainly no time to add more greenhouse gases or deplete biodiversity." Mass human-induced extinctions could make things worse and be an added cause of climate change.

Scientists may be worried, but some economists behave like ostriches. Professor William Nordhaus of Yale University, Nobel Prize winner for economics, calculated that the US could afford to spend no more than two percent of GDP to combat global warming because that was the value of the agriculture and forestry sectors which would be affected by climate change. His calculation formed the basis of US negotiations at 1992 Rio World Summit (though, in fact, the US spends nothing like this figure). He ignored the fact that people cannot survive without food, so the monetary value of agriculture would greatly increase if it were seriously harmed by changed climatic conditions. This would be amusing if it did not demonstrate the quality of economic advice on which great nations rely.

Economists then asked "is it worth doing anything?" Cost/benefit studies were carried out. Economists and statisticians made all sorts of assumptions on the extent and effects of climate change in areas that scientists say are impossible to predict. They came up with the suggestion that we should do nothing about global warming, just let it rip and pay for re-settling the displaced, it would be cheaper that way. One of the assumptions had to be the cost of death, as a lot of people would die. David Pearce, a leading British economist, insisted that one European or US life is worth 15 Chinese or Indian lives. He was right, of course, within the framework of a discipline that treats people as economic units. He just demonstrated one of the grotesque failings of mainstream flat earth economics.

How might we be affected?

A fast temperature change does not allow time for species to adapt. If that occurred, whole biological systems would collapse. If farmers cannot rely on weather patterns the food system is threatened. If the land-based West Antarctic ice sheet were to dislodge, ocean levels would rise by six metres flooding many cities and much of the developed world's infrastructure including many nuclear reactors. It could be the end of civilisation. These are scenarios, not predictions. Almost all predictions are wrong and the actuality will be different. The economists and statisticians mentioned above made the mistake of treating predictions as immutable. Action should not be based on predictions but on systematic thinking that brings our activities into harmony with the processes of a unique planet.

The health of coral reefs has been likened to the miner's canary – if the canary tips off its perch the miner is in trouble – and corals are bleaching around the world. Krill, the staple food of the Antarctic, is depleting. Early springs are leading to a mismatch between the peak food demands of birds and the availability of insects. Some tropical diseases, like malaria and West Nile Virus, are spreading out of their normal areas. Glaciers are receding. Unusual flooding has happened in China, Bangladesh, India, and Africa. Hurricane Mitch killed 18,000 people. But this is only a small sample of the effects of climate change. **It is happening due to the rise in temperature of only 0.6°C. What will happen when this warming is multiplied by five or ten?**

The last word can go to the insurance industry, which is the one business that cannot afford to ignore what is happening. With present trends, insured losses will outstrip global GDP in 60 years; we cannot spend all our wealth on disasters, so the crunch will come much earlier even if climate change does not speed up. Already some weather events are not insurable. The industry is pressing governments to **do something**. Quickly.

Fossil energy, dams, traffic, aeroplanes, fish and industrial agriculture attract subsidies of $2,000 billion a year worldwide. In the words of the Earth Council: "the world is spending hundreds of billions of dollars annually to subsidise its own destruction."

Comparative CO_2 emissions in grams per tonne-kilometre:

Boat	30 g/t-k
Rail	41 g/t-k
Road	207 g/t-k
Air	1,206 g/t-k

Trade-related transportation by air is one of the fastest growing sources of greenhouse gas emissions but it is not covered by the Kyoto protocol and aviation fuel is not even taxed – a £9bn annual subsidy by the British chancellor for the destruction of the planet.

The British government has funny priorities, it reduced the railway network by 60% and then privatised it so that it is now among the most expensive and unreliable services in the world.

God's Last Offer
Ed Ayres 1999

Europe Cooling

the last days of our green and pleasant land?

The British rather like the idea of a warmer climate but serious climate change may deny them. Ironically, global warming may cause the regional cooling of Europe in our lifetime.

Most scare stories relate to the south, like the 150 million environmental migrants that may be created in Asia by climate instability. It is ocean currents that might harm Europe.

Ocean currents have a critical impact on climate. The deep water of the 'Atlantic conveyor', which drives the Gulf Stream, takes about a thousand years to circulate at low level around the world, so it was assumed that these currents provide long-term stability. But recently this assumption has been put in doubt. The first shock came when currents in the Mediterranean went into reverse in just one year. Then the deep sea current between Greenland and Norway did the same. During part of the last interglacial period average temperatures in Greenland moved up and down by as much as 7°C in a decade, probably due to the switching on and off of Atlantic ocean currents. Although average world temperatures have only risen 0.6°C in recent years, some arctic weather stations now show warming of 5°C. The thickness of some ice sheets has halved, and their area has reduced by 16%. Strange things are already happening in polar regions.

When ice forms from seawater in the Arctic it leaves the salt behind. The resulting cold, heavy, salty water drops to the ocean floor, creating 'pumps' that draw surface water, the Gulf Stream, and drive the Atlantic conveyor. The water in these pumps is now getting less saline, therefore lighter, because less water is freezing. It is also being joined by fresh salt-free water from melting icebergs. And it is getting warmer. If this process continues, a critical point will be reached and the pumps will stop.

The Gulf Stream brings warm water from the tropics to Britain keeping us at a pleasant temperature. Without it, our climate would resemble that of Labrador or parts of Siberia. **Our agriculture would be destroyed.** Britain plc would be found only in history books.

In 1997 some scientists said that this could happen in our lifetime. The US National Academy of Sciences now confirms that the change is "likely", adding that change occurs as when "the slowly increasing pressure of a finger eventually flips a switch and turns off the light".

The top political issue, globally, is to find a mechanism for phasing out the use of fossil fuels. Yet our government is only concerned with short term electoral issues and sacked Michael Meacher, the only minister prepared to draw attention to the priorities of the real world.

The pumps are powered by high salt concentrations near the waters surface. Melting ice dilutes the salt and weakens the pump.

As the pumps weaken, the current slows down and may suddenly switch off.

The system depends on so-called 'natural pumps' around Greenland which draw warm water up towards northwest Europe and send cold water back southwards.

The Gulf Stream brings warm water from the tropics as part of a worldwide network of ocean currents.

Rio and Kyoto

let's put it off until tomorrow

At the 1992 Earth Summit in Rio, three requirements for action on climate change were clearly set out:

- "To achieve **stabilisation of greenhouse gas** concentrations in the atmosphere at a level that could prevent dangerous anthropogenic interference with the climate system" (Article 2).

- The Parties should "protect the climate system for the benefit of humankind **on the basis of equity**" (Article 3.1).

- Measures "should be **cost-effective** so as to ensure global benefits at lowest possible cost" (Article 3.3). This hints at emission trading.

No agreement has got near to meeting these requirements. The urgent need to address critical problems with the climate, that brought so many heads of state to Rio, was soon forgotten. Due to intense pressure from oil and coal companies it was not until 1995 that the Intergovernmental Panel on Climate Change (IPCC) was able to issue the unanimous, if minimalist, statement that "the balance of evidence suggests a discernible human influence on climate." Twelve years after Rio, the 'balance of evidence' suggests that there has been no discernible influence on human-caused greenhouse gas emissions despite international conferences, hundreds of select committees and millions of bureaucratic hours. Emissions continue to rise and global warming has followed the IPCC's worst-case scenario.

At Kyoto, in 1997, a hundred countries, mainly of the North, agreed to reduce their greenhouse gas emissions to 5.2% below 1990 levels within 15 years; but China and India, which have the fastest growth in pollution, were not included. This was totally inadequate to meet Rio's first requirement, to stabilise concentrations in the atmosphere. In addition, each country was given a quota based on current level of emissions (called 'grand-fathering'). This blatantly breached Rio's second requirement, for equity, since the more damage a country had caused in the past, the more it would be allowed to pollute in the future. The Kyoto protocol was finally signed by 178 countries representing 95.7% of the world's population.

Only the United States walked away from the treaty thus giving its businesses an unfair advantage. Europe should encourage the US to sign by imposing trade sanctions, as sanctioned by the WTO for achieving a level playing field.

We can expect climate instability and collapsed biological systems. Millions may become environmental migrants; deserts may replace farmland; low-lying agriculture may be engulfed; epidemics may spread. Pacific states are already facing inundation, and their sentiment was well expressed at Kyoto by the President of Nauru: **"The willful destruction, with foreknowledge, of entire countries and cultures represents an unspeakable crime against humanity."** If calamitous climate change occurs, as now seems probable, the slow and inadequate action by the rich minority nations will overshadow all other acts of barbarism in the history of humankind.

Can the Kyoto protocol help? It is a step in the right direction but more is necessary if Rio's three urgent requirements are to be met.

Trading pollution

Although trading pollution sounds bizarre it was spectacularly successful in the US for reducing sulphur emissions under the tradable permit scheme of the 1991 Clean Air Act. Most human activity pollutes in some way. Defecation pollutes, but is a part of life's cycle. In moderation burning wood is not harmful. Plants and trees emit carbon dioxide when they die but this helps other plants to grow. Emission rights should be traded only if the aggregate total of these emissions rights is low enough not to cause harm. Europe has started a trading scheme for industrial emissions.

The Carbon War
Jeremy Leggett 1999

Uncertainties

Uncertainties enable bureaucrats to extend negotiations indefinitely and avoid effective action (while being treated as experts and having secure career structures). And the climate is full of uncertainties. Forests absorb CO2 (good, though only for a time) while their heat absorption in areas that would otherwise be covered in snow causes warming (bad). Soil traps CO2 but this will be released when the earth warms. Small particles (aerosols) have a short term cooling effect so screen the warming trend. Methane has not been fed into climate models and could be exacerbated by a hydrogen economy. Then negotiators come up with 'clean development mechanisms,' 'joint implementation' and other complications to keep the arguments running.

Many scientists are furious with the bureaucrats and say that the problem is too urgent for these quibbles, the only sure way to contain damage is to reduce emissions. John Houghton, former chair of the IPPC working party, describes climate change as a weapon of mass destruction.

Historic Responsibility

Scientists are now able to define the amount of carbon dioxide that has been emitted from each country in the past. This enables allocation of emission rights to be based not only on population but also on a country's total liability for damage, past and present. Low emitting countries could insist on this basis for setting allocations.

Glofs

As Himalayan glaciers melt they form lakes held in by packed ice. These lakes, some of them over a square mile in area and 300 feet deep, are getting bigger. At some stage the ice dams will burst and a wall of water will destroy everything in its path – settlements, bridges and dams. These 'glofs' (glacial lake outburst floods) will affect Nepal, Bhutan, India and Pakistan. Will the industrial world, which has grown rich on its profligate use of fossil fuels, undertake massive and urgent remedial action to reduce the levels of the lakes? On present trends their response is to say, "Tough! We need to burn more fossil fuels; how else can we maintain our standard of living?"

Contraction & Convergence

the solution to link survival and justice

*"We hold these truths to be self-evident,
that all men are created equal."*
US Declaration of Independence 1776

These two statements are logical and fair. They are perhaps the only issues relating to climate negotiations that really matter. But they did not form part of the Kyoto protocol.

Six months before Kyoto, the US Senate voted unanimously against signing any agreement that did not include **all countries.** (the Byrd Hagel resolution).

African, Indian and Chinese delegates said that carbon emission allocations should be **proportional to a nation's population.** "Emission control standards" said the Chinese delegate, Song Jian, "should be formulated on a per-capita basis. According to the UN Charter everybody is born equal and has inalienable rights to enjoy modern technological civilisation."

The Global Commons Institute had prepared a framework for Kyoto called Contraction & Convergence that was consistent with both these statements and met the three requirements formulated five years earlier by heads of state at the Rio Earth Summit. Developing nations accepted it as the basis for agreement in 1997 and a senior US negotiator called it "the only game in town." It is also starkly simple.

Contraction: we must obviously contract emissions to a level that will not destabilise the climate. At present scientists think that a 60% contraction on 1990 figures is essential, but further cuts may become necessary.

Convergence: all nations will converge to an equal-per-inhabitant allocation of the right to emit greenhouse gases by an agreed date. Countries can trade their allocations.

Contraction & Convergence is as simple as that. But it has huge implications, in the way that fundamental concepts like 'democracy' are simple but have huge implications.

Everyone in the world is dependent on the atmosphere, it is a 'global common'. If it can only absorb a certain amount of greenhouse gases without harm then it is only fair that we should all have an equal ration of the limited amount it can absorb – equal emission rights. Not every country nor every person will use the exact allocation but, if the allocations can be traded, frugal people and frugal countries will benefit. Imagine the Indian peasant receiving his or her Emission Right coupons each month which he or she can sell – a basic income.

Why should one person be allowed to pollute more than another?

Contraction of greenhouse gas emissions is essential for our survival, and Contraction & Convergence (C&C) provides the market incentives to achieve this. Rich nations that emit excessively will have the *incentive* to reduce their emissions as quickly as possible in order to reduce the number of emission-rights they need to buy. Poor nations that do not use their full allocation will have the *incentive* to limit their emissions in order to retain emission-rights for sale. By providing incentives it avoids the pitfalls of a purely regulatory approach or an approach based on horse-trading between nations.

C&C is not totally fair on poor countries that could argue they deserve higher allocations because the rich have already caused so much damage through excessive emissions. They could also argue, with justification, that equal-per-capita allocations should be applied immediately, without a convergence period. But compromise is the essence of politics, and it appears that, at this stage, they might be prepared to compromise if the convergence period is short, say a decade. They may change their minds if the rich continue to refuse equal use of a global common.

Equal-per-capita allocations to emit a certain amount of carbon dioxide would result in money flowing from the rich (who use more than their share) to the poor (who have allocations to sell) as of right, not as arbitrary aid. Contraction & Convergence is therefore not only a framework for reducing global carbon emissions to a sustainable level, it is also a market mechanism that will reverse the persistent tendency to inequality. It links the desperate need to stop global warming to the equally desperate need to reduce inequality: survival linked to justice.

The Royal Commission on Environmental Pollution says: "The UK should be prepared to accept the C&C principle as the basis for international agreement on reducing greenhouse gas emissions." The equivalent body advised the German government that "emission rights should be allocated according to the C&C approach". President Chirac has welcomed the proposal.

We are at a critical moment in the earth's history, a time when humanity must choose either to continue on its present disastrous course or to live within the earth's physical limits and move towards an equitable society.

Don't leave it to rich nations. The majority nations tried to establish this approach at Kyoto in 1997 but the principles were sidelined and ignored. History so far shows that rich countries have consistently put their own interests above environmental or humanitarian concerns. If the rich retain control of negotiations they will probably insist on a long contraction period even though this threatens their own, and all humanity's, survival.

China, India, Brazil together with other countries that represent the majority of the global population, the G21, should take leadership of C&C immediately, agree on a timeframe for contraction and a rapid rate for convergence to equal-per-capita allocations, say ten years, and assert their democratic vote. Rich countries say they believe in democracy; their claim must now be put to the test. This may be the last chance to avert climatic and social chaos. This could be the defining decision for the future of humanity.

www.gci.org.uk
Global Commons Institute

DTQs

towards equity in each country

A fair allocation of carbon rights could work locally. Everyone, however poor, would then have something of value either to use herself or to sell – a basic income.

"A good month – only took car out four times and walked to work every day – swipe-card used only a quarter of carbon quota – £350 credited to statement." Diary note

Under the Domestic Tradable Quota (DTQ) system you would receive your quota of Special Emission Rights (SERs) each month. The amount of carbon fuel (petrol or gas) you use determines the amount of carbon dioxide you emit. Your smart-card carbon-account would be debited whenever you use fuel with a carbon content, for example at the filling station or when paying the gas bill. There would be a central register at QuotaCo.

People who use less than their quota would sell their surplus on the open market to people that use more than theirs.

Britain has a target for reducing greenhouse gas emissions. By issuing the appropriate number of SERs it would *know* that this target would be met without hoping that taxes, subsidies and regulations would achieve the desired result.

Once the carbon units have been issued the market would operate. The family that has a well-insulated house and does not drive a car would have carbon units to sell, while the chief executive who must fly his private jet would need to buy units. This would not interfere with people's freedom to choose their lifestyle. The government could then concentrate on measures to relieve rural deprivation, to help people insulate their homes and other social benefits.

The system would have four results:

- Everyone would have a commodity that can be sold, providing him or her with a basic income. This would reduce the need for arbitrary social measures.

- There would be a built-in tendency towards financial equality because money would flow from those who choose a lavish, carbon-polluting, lifestyle to those who don't.

- There would be an incentive for businesses as well as individuals to reduce carbon use. Excess users would reduce their use of carbon in order not to buy allocations. The frugal would keep their use of carbon low to have more allocations to sell.

- The demand for non-carbon energy and products would increase and companies, because of the need to buy units, would reduce carbon use wherever possible.

The quota would initially be close to present emissions of carbon dioxide but gradually reduce, allowing time for businesses and society to adjust. After Kyoto's 12.5% reduction of emissions has been achieved, more reductions will be necessary to bring global emissions down to a sustainable level as set out in the Contraction and Convergence framework.

The system has been designed to work with smart cards but this could not apply to all countries. In poor countries these units (Special Emission Rights) would be distributed as coupons that could be exchanged for money in local agencies. In India this could be administered through the post offices that handle food-relief allocation coupons. Everyone would have an equal right so corruption would be difficult. Thus a basic income would be available for the poorest in society, throughout the world.

A country's performance would be monitored. Countries that fail to distribute transparently and fully would be penalised by reduction of the number of Special Emission Rights they receive.

Tribes

Freedom from constant anxiety and toil, as provided by the DTQ, could meet the evolved needs of human society. Animals survive and cooperate socially in ways that evolved over eons of time. Wolves have packs, fish have shoals and bees have hives. We humans also have social organisation built into our psyche through three million years of evolution – as tribes. Only in the last few thousand years have tribes been replaced by hierarchical organisation. Tribes have been exterminated by 'civilisation' wherever the two come into contact. Free access to land, water and food, enjoyed by tribal society, has been denied to civilised society. Instead of accepting human reality, which was the basis of tribal sustainability, civilisation's religions have campaigned for human nature to be changed. Even the word 'tribal' is vilified in civilisation's languages. Not surprisingly, civilisation has been achieved at terrible cost to the majority.

With the basic income provided by DTQs, **people can be freed from the requirement to drag rocks up the pyramids of the élite.** We can survive and cooperate within stress-free associations – the new tribes.

The carbon content of fuels is:

Petrol	2.3 CU per litre
Diesel	2.4 CU per litre
Natural gas	0.2 CU per kilowatt-hour
Night electricity	0.6 CU per kilowatt-hour
Day electricity	0.7 CU per kilowatt-hour

CU = kilograms of carbon dioxide released

Enlightened self-interest.

In 1998, DuPont announced its intention to cut its heat-trapping gas by 65% by 2010. In 2001, the company reached, and surpassed, that goal, nine years ahead of schedule. Since 1990, DuPont has succeeded in holding its energy use at these levels. The company attributes a \$1.65 billion savings to its programme over the past decade.

Ishmael *and*
Beyond Civilisation
Daniel Quinn
1997 and 1999

www.dtqs.org
The Lean Economy Institute

The Future of Oil

who's fooling whom? – and why?

solar energy captured

← extend this line for five miles

solar energy extracted

Draw a line five miles long to represent the millions of years during which solar energy has been captured and laid down in the earth's crust in the form of coal, gas and oil. Then put a blip in it. That blip represents the time we have taken to extract and use this embodied energy. We are half way through the blip.

These fuels have given us a material standard of living that previous generations could not have imagined in their wildest dreams. Coal gave Britain an Empire and the US gained global power by being the first to exploit oil. Scientific progress would have been stultified without these fuels. But we treat them as a permanent part of the economy. They are not. **Our grandchildren will have to manage without them.**

M. King Hubbert said, in 1956, that oil extraction in the US would peak after 15 years and then decline, never to revive. At the time extraction was relentlessly increasing and oil companies said he was mad. In 1971 US oil production duly peaked, as he predicted, and has declined ever since in spite of a desperate hunt supported by the most sophisticated equipment in the world. The US, though it started with 10% of the world's oil (for 4.3% of world's population) now uses a quarter of the world's oil production and imports two-thirds of this. World oil is following the same pattern of discovery and extraction, and we are at the peak.

The history of discovery is well documented and, obviously, more oil cannot be produced than is discovered. US mainland (48 states) oil discoveries

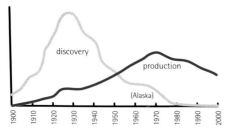

United States discovery and production of oil
(vertical scale as for world x10)

World discovery and production of oil

peaked in 1930, 40 years before production peaked. World oil discoveries peaked in the 1960s and new discoveries are gradually getting fewer and smaller. New fields will, of course, be found and each will grab the headlines for a time. But they cannot change the overall pattern.

The total amount of conventional oil in the world (already used, reserves and yet-to-find) has been about 2,000 Gb (billion barrels) and about half has been extracted. We are now on a plateau where the amount of oil that can be produced is not much more than the amount in demand. High oil prices have always brought recession so the world may dip in and out of recession for a few years. But, within a decade, the amount of oil that can be produced will drop, never to recover, and this could trigger a global recession or depression.

For a hundred years the global economy has grown, serviced by oil. The world economy has determined how much oil is produced. This is about to go into reverse. Oil will determine the global economy unless or until renewable sources can provide adequate energy. Everything – trade, manufacturing, services, exchange – will be measured not by money but by its use of energy. Energy will become the new currency.

President Carter, 1976-80, was aware of the dangers of oil dependence. He said that we must not find ourselves in the position of having to fight wars to seize other people's oil; a couple of decades of transition to renewable energy sources would ensure the stability and future of America without destabilising the rest of the world. He put in place incentives to achieve solar-heated homes, windmill-powered communities and fuel-alternatives to petrol. Ronald Reagan, on achieving office, immediately removed Carter's solar panels from the roof of the White House and repealed his tax incentives. The US dependence on oil imports now results in military action wherever there are significant oil reserves.

Saudi Arabia, with the biggest reserves, had a US-army presence on its sacred land, a US-trained defence force for its rulers, a US fleet in the Gulf and, under the 'Woolsey Plan', it could be broken up and a US protectorate installed in the oil-rich area. Iraq, with the second biggest reserves, was invaded and subjected to military occupation. The Caspian has significant reserves so, through the Afghan war, the US established permanent military bases in all Central Asian republics – Secretary of State Colin Powell said "America will have a continuing interest and presence in Central Asia of a kind that we could not have dreamed of before." Iran is being threatened as it could close the Straight of Hormuz, cutting off the Gulf. Venezuela has the largest reserves outside the Middle East. Through control of world oil the US aims to be in a position to control the policy of any rival such as China, Japan, Europe or Russia.

For some incomprehensible reason we encourage the wasteful use of oil. Huge subsidies are given to oil-dependent industrial agriculture; air travel is free of tax, and the use of road transport is encouraged by the provision of new roads.

Does oil benefit a country? Angola has vast reserves but its people do not benefit. 'Commercial confidentiality' keeps dealings opaque, making corruption inevitable. Oil executives live in an opulent fenced town with no local contact and fly to offshore rigs – a typical arrangement for foreign exploitation of Africa. The government gets so much income from oil that it has little interest in the domestic economy. Luanda, the capital, is the most expensive city in the world after Tokyo yet two-thirds of its people have no access to clean drinking water and Angola languishes at the bottom of the UN Human Development Index.

China's oil imports increased 30% in the first ten months of 2003.

Before the Wells Run Dry
Feasta 2003

Hydrogen Economy

the future of energy

"Yes, my friends, I believe that water will one day be employed as fuel, that hydrogen and oxygen which constitute it, used singly or together, will furnish an inexhaustible source of heat and light, of an intensity of which coal is not capable."
Jules Verne, The Mysterious Island, 1874

Iceland could be the first country in the world to emit no greenhouse gases. It may demonstrate what a hydrogen economy looks like.

For 50 years Iceland has been using its plentiful hydro and geothermal electricity to heat buildings and to extract hydrogen from water using an electrolytic process. It is beginning to use offshore wind turbines as well. The process can now be reversed. Hydrogen can be combined with oxygen to become water again and, in the process, drive a fuel cell motor. Hydrogen will be produced at filling stations using renewable electricity sources. First the bus fleet will be powered by fuel cell motors, then private cars and then the fishing fleet. Then Iceland will be totally independent of fossil fuels. Bragi Arnason, who first had the idea in 1978, points to the advantage of Iceland as the pilot country: "It's easy to introduce a new technology in a small society," he says "because if it goes wrong it's less difficult to fix it. Then you take the lessons you've learned here and apply them to larger societies."

The programme in Iceland may not be complete until at least 2040. And that is just one small country that has all the advantages and is well on the way. Others haven't started. How long will it take to put a global infrastructure for hydrogen in place? How long to replace machinery with fuel cell motors? There will be a shortage of energy for decades after oil supplies peak and decline.

Hydrogen is the most abundant element in the universe and fuels the sun. Politicians like to find easy ways out of energy problems, and they can tell OPEC to keep oil prices low or they will change to renewable fuels. What's the problem?

The energy you can extract from hydrogen is less than the energy you put into making it – that is the second law of thermodynamics – so using gas, coal or oil to make it is more damaging than using these fuels themselves. Only solar, wind or water-flow technologies that produce renewable electricity (or nuclear, but that has other problems) can avoid greenhouse gas emissions. Then there are problems once it is made. Hydrogen reacts with metals making containers brittle, it evaporates even from within a container, it seeps, it has low energy content against volume so has to be stored under pressure, endangering explosion; or it can be liquefied but this needs constant refrigeration. And though it is difficult to transport, it needs to be available at every filling station and at every airport. Then there are suggestions that extensive use of hydrogen might damage the ozone layer, and it could add to global warming by releasing methane in the troposphere.

But the biggest problem will be the electricity required. To meet our present energy needs with compressed hydrogen for cars and liquified hydrogen for aeroplanes would require three times the electricity we generate at present. A hydrogen economy must be accompanied by a drastic reduction in our use of energy.

As with all major new technologies research will take time and precaution is necessary. Perhaps the greatest danger is haste but haste may be forced on us when the energy gap looms.

California has got the message. The National Fuel Cell Research Centre has been deluged with calls from businesses asking for its advice because of rocketing electricity bills and mains supply failure. The State is offering half a billion dollars. Manufacturers are developing stationary fuel cell equipment, small enough to carry on a lorry and capable of serving individual buildings. The power will be generated and used locally and there is no need or intention to connect it to the State grid. 21% of California's power will come from wind and photovoltaics using fuel cells within 10 years.

Nuclear Power

too hot to handle

The process starts with uranium, U, the heaviest naturally occurring element. It is also the only one that has 'fissile' content. There are 140 parts of U-238 (238 neutrons) for every one part of U-235 and it is the latter that is fissile – which means that its nucleus can be split as nuclear fuel. The uranium is 'enriched' by removing much of the U-238 to achieve a high proportion of the fissile material; this results in a large amount of 'depleted' U-238 uranium (DU), an extremely dense radioactive by-product that is given to the military, to civil aviation and to train manufacturers. Fission takes place when the U-235 nucleus captures (absorbs) a neutron; the nucleus then becomes unstable and splits into two fragments referred to as 'fission products' that are normally radioactive isotopes like strontium-90, caesium-137, iodine-131 etc. The split releases neutrons, which initiate further fission in neighbouring U-235 nuclei, and a chain reaction is set up, controlled in a reactor, un-controlled in a bomb. The fission process also releases a few neutrons that are not absorbed so that the mass of the fission products is slightly less than the mass of the original nucleus. It is this tiny difference in mass (m) that releases energy (E), and when multiplied by the speed of light (c) squared (Einstein's famous equation $E = mc2$), it is a lot of energy. In the chain reaction the fissile uranium undergoes radioactive decay, first to neptunium, then to plutonium. So, when uranium is used in a nuclear reactor plutonium inevitably accumulates as a by-product. Plutonium is another fissile material but it is man-made and only found naturally in minute traces.

Pluto is the mythical God of Hell and plutonium is named after him. It has virtually no peaceful uses apart from small amounts in 'breeder' and mixed-fuel thermal reactors. It is among the most toxic substances in existence, inhale a minute particle and you are likely to die of lung cancer, ingest some and you may die of bone or liver cancer.

Plutonium comes from 450 civilian nuclear reactors in 29 countries, and from dismantled nuclear weapons in the US and Russia.

Reprocessing plants in just a few countries separate plutonium from reactor fuel. The plutonium is then sent back to the country of origin by ships, air, railways and road. The transport of plutonium is a gift to terrorists. The danger is so great that democracy in countries with stockpiles may be seriously undermined because of the need for intense and active security. Sellafield has the biggest stockpile in the world. A cupful of plutonium attached to a conventional high explosive could render a city uninhabitable. Whatever the future of nuclear power, reprocessing should be stopped immediately.

Uranium, plutonium and most fission products go through a complex process of decay (including americium which cannot be screened by protective suits) that lasts hundreds of thousands of years while giving off radioactivity. Extremely low doses of radioactivity can cause cancers and birth defects, where the genome is affected (granite gives off some radioactivity but it undergoes a different decay process that is less dangerous).

There is no such thing as a safe level of radiation so it must not be allowed to increase in the environment. Industry scientists say that the best way to dispose of high-level radioactive waste is to turn it into glass, put it in stainless steel containers, leave it for 50 years to cool and then bury it in stable geological strata. Environmental scientists say that there are no stable geological strata and they recommend perpetual supervised storage above ground. No method for safe disposal of nuclear waste is known. Then there are growing tonnes of lower-level waste, and nuclear reactors have to be dismantled and probably covered in earth – to resemble the mounds that Odysseus raised for the honoured dead. One wonders what future civilisations will make of these tumuli with their ghostly and ghastly magical properties.

Most nuclear power plants keep waste pools that are more vulnerable to sabotage than reactor cores. 70 tons of plutonium is stored in insecure buildings at Sellafield and a major accident could write off the north of England. In the US, highly active waste is dumped in a desert area where it can leach into aquifers. If wealthy nations can't be trusted to dispose of the stuff safely, what can one expect of poor nations?

Can we let this continue? The production of radioactive wastes with their dangerous legacy to future generations, the proliferation of nuclear weapons, the exposure of populations to additional ionising radiation, nuclear accidents, nuclear terrorism, nuclear war, restrictions on civic freedom, are so frightening and unacceptable that nuclear power should be phased out altogether. Even if we think we can survive the dangers oursel-ves, can we inflict these problems on our children?

We should not be asking how to meet humanity's energy demands but how can humanity live within the planet's constraints without causing harm?

- Nuclear warfare is now likely. Unstoppable Sunburn and Onyx missiles of Russian origin, able to vapourise an aircraft carrier or a small state, are widely distributed in the Middle East and Asia. And the US is developing mini-nukes (quarter Hiroshimas) and bunker-busters (ten Hiroshimas) for 'tactical' use.

- **Depleted uranium (DU)** is a radioactive waste product of nuclear reactors and is given without charge to arms manufacturers because that is easier than storing it. It is so dense that it penetrates tank armour. It is used for bunker-busters and cluster bombs. It burns on impact, releasing radioactive dust particles. US army manuals warn "contamination will make food and water unsafe for consumption." Children play on destroyed tanks that UK survey teams will only touch in full-body radiation suits. It will be active for the life of the planet causing cancer, kidney disease and birth defects. Half the veterans of the 1991 Gulf War, where DU was used, are either dead or sick, their symptoms matching those of visitors to Hiroshima after the atom bomb. Some of the veterans' children are born without arms but with swollen torsos and shrivelled legs, just like many children in Iraq. Afghanistan, Baghdad and the Balkans are contaminated. The UN describes DU as a weapon of indiscriminate use that continues to kill after hostilities and therefore infringes the Geneva Convention. DU is beginning to be used in the civilian manufacture of trains and aircraft.

In Iraq a mother's first agonising query about her newborn baby is: "is it normal?"

The Arms Trade

disreputable and deluded

> *"Few of us can easily surrender our belief that society must somehow make sense. The thought that the state has lost its mind is intolerable, and so the evidence has to be denied."*
> Arthur Miller

The trade in death and destruction used to be easy to understand. Arms manufacturers were workshops for national armed forces to provide each nation with the means of aggression or defence and to sell weapons to any nation that lacked an industry of its own. Up to a point this is still the public perception. It is wrong. The big arms traders are now multinational corporations.

Is BAEs a US or a British company? It started life as a British Aerospace but dropped the British for B (like BT, BA and BP). It owns former US companies and claims to be "the only European arms company that is truly big in the US and the only US arms company that is truly big in Europe." At the same time BAEs wants the UK government to believe that it is British so that Tony Blair will continue to promote it when trotting around the world. But the US accounts for over half of the world's arms expenditure and Congress could, at any time, decide that a company should be excluded for national security reasons. The commercial logic is that BAEs will become a fully US company. **The aim of the arms trade, of course, is not to serve any national interest but to maximise shareholder value.**

Why should the government support employment that makes products of no real utility? It would be more profitable and less damaging to support cocaine or cigarette companies. But it is not about employment. "The economic costs of reducing defence exports are relatively small and largely one-off," said the UK government's Defence Sales Committee in its 2002 report, adding that the loss would lead to an increase in civilian jobs over a five-year period. The arms industry is the most heavily subsidised sector of the British economy after agriculture.

The UN Security Council's five permanent members, who should be aiming to reduce conflict, are the biggest arms traders and all of their governments actively encourage the manufacture and sale of weapons. They should be banned from membership.

The arms trade thrives on conflict. If it can encourage an arms race between two countries so much the better. And governments help. When India and Pakistan threatened nuclear confrontation, Blair, Prescott and Straw each visited the area to promote arms sales to both sides. Britain continues to arm Indonesia in spite of its atrocities in Aceh. The US armed the Vietnamese (against Japan), Iraq (against Iran), Iran (against Iraq), Osama bin Laden (against Russia) and even the Taliban. And the encouragement of arms sales with loans and export guarantees to poor countries is one of the chief reasons for their crippling debt.

Politicians fear losing votes if soldiers' lives are lost, so they have to be kept at a safe distance from harm. Smart and precision-laser-guided missiles are delivered from highly complex planes travelling at great speed miles away, too far to recognise wedding celebrations, and nine out of ten victims are civilians – not usually western citizens so their lives are of no concern to our politicians. The arms trade ensures that these weapons are soon superseded by more sophisticated ones (good for business) and the outdated weapons are sold to unsuspecting states, encouraging further cycles of violence.

A language of euphemism has replaced the horrors of war. Leaders that declare war and those that profit from selling weapons of war are detached from the results of their actions; they don't describe the screams of a child having her arm amputated without anaesthetic.

How can 'decent' people and 'civilised' nations engage in such a disreputable activity whose end product is only mutilation, death and destruction?

www.caat.org.uk
Campaign Against Arms Trade

Weapons of War

war is no longer an option

"Nine out of ten Americans exterminated." This would be a dramatic headline if any television or newspaper survived to carry it. But it actually happened in the 16th century.

In 1527, 170 Spaniards walked into an army of 100,000. Pizarro captured Atahuallpa, the Inca were routed and piles of gold were transferred to Europe. Although the Spaniards' initial success was due to sharp steel weapons, horses, helmets, body armour and deception, the extermination that followed was due to germs. Evolution ensures that organisms develop resistance to harmful bacteria and viruses, but smallpox was new to America and Americans had evolved no resistance. So smallpox, an unintended bio-weapon, decimated Americans.

Most people live in poor countries. The majority nations, once colonies, became 'young nations with a bright future.' But now the wealthy minority glowers at what it sees as a risk-prone zone, a breeding ground for crisis and terrorism, suffering from epidemics, over-population, desertification, violence, and corruption. However these majority nations hold the minerals, the crops, the genetic richness and the potential markets that the rich minority nations covet and plunder.

In the last century, nuclear weapons created apocalyptic dangers that are still with us. In the new century we have new causes for conflict, new targets and new weapons.

● A third of the world's 'natural wealth' has been lost due to over-consumption. So scarcity of resources, more than ideological difference, is now the main **cause** of conflict. Countries are invaded to secure commodities like oil. Governments, weakened by globalisation, cannot protect their diamonds and old-growth timber from plunder by corporations and non-state groups – and the free flow of capital across borders allows these groups to amass fortunes and obtain weapons. Water shortages, worsened by industrial farming and grandiose dams, cause escalating disputes between and even within countries. Land degradation and a changing climate each give rise to mass migrations that exacerbate these conflicts. The lifestyle of the rich, made possible by resources taken from poor countries, is widely seen by the poor on mass media, provoking anger and envy.

● It has become difficult to locate **targets**. The US and Britain could lob bombs from a safe distance into Iraq, bring it to its knees by causing starvation and disease through sanctions before invading. But an individual like Osama bin Laden, or an intransigent carrying a handbag with unpleasant contents, is more elusive.

● **Weapons** are new. The rich apply the world's wealth to sophisticated weapons technology. Poor states can now get access to missiles carrying radioactive waste. Non-state groups can obtain lethal chemicals. Computer viruses can be sent over the ether. Microbes can be modified by simply adding key genes to close relatives to make strains resembling Ebola or the 1918 flu that killed forty million people; thousands of laboratories around the world have the necessary equipment and the virus can be spread by an infected individual simply walking through a crowded city. A single individual with military connections sent packets of anthrax to US politicians in 2002. And nanobots may literally eat people alive.

War in an electronic, nuclear, chemical, and biological age is no longer an option. Germs brought the first American civilisations to an end. Ours may end with President Bush's policy of domination, bin Laden's terrorism or Blair's warmongering. If we think war, if war is our consciousness, we face catastrophe. Nothing less than a new consciousness is necessary.

The 'frangible' bullet is new and horrible. It explodes inside the body creating untreatable wounds. Its manufacturers are saying to the US in effect "pay us to help kill your enemies or we'll help your enemies to kill you".

In Afghanistan 70,000 cluster bomblets, the size of cricket balls, await children's games. Cluster bombs are sold openly to anyone at arms fairs with an explanation that the bomblets are, in reality, landmines.

Costa Rica has a better approach. In 1948 José Figueres, President of Costa Rica, disbanded the army. The military budget was given to education and health. The banks, insurance, all utilities and the railways were nationalised. A wealth tax and a social security system were introduced. Women and Caribbean immigrants were given the right to vote. But it was not an easy ride. The US tried to overthrow Figueres in 1950 and twice attempted to assassinate him. A century-old dispute with Nicaragua

It's safer down here

over the use of the San Juan river flared up in 1998 but was settled after two years of patient negotiation without resort to arms. Significantly, it is the only country in the region that has not been invaded or used as a base by the US.

Costa Rica is now democratic, relatively rich, and regularly makes the top 50 in the UN Human Development Index. The educated populace makes it an attractive country for investment. But 'economic violence' may yet destroy the dream. Privatisations, following pressure from the IMF, recently caused widespread rioting. According to the former president, "Costa Ricans have cultivated a civilised spirit, a spirit antithetical to militarisation and violence, capable of finding peaceful solutions to conflicts and respectful of the rights of others. In the absence of weapons with which to impose an idea, the only weapon left is reason. Today, people such as myself have become fully convinced that **a country that organises an army becomes its own jailer.**"

Losing Control
Paul Rogers 2001

Tools for Peace

alternatives to violence are possible

Some women of Wajir, in Kenya, put an end to clan warfare. The joining test of their group was "if my clan were to kill your relatives, would you still work with me for peace? If you can't say 'yes', don't join the group." After many stormy meetings with the elders, conferences and active involvement with a multitude of groups, peaceful life has been restored. One innovation was the 'Rapid Response Team' consisting of elders, youth and women who rushed to intervene wherever violence flared up. An elder commented "most of what was accomplished was done by people with a heart for peace."

To achieve peace we need to think peace. We need peace consciousness from the bottom-up and from the top-down. A Peace Council should replace the UN Security Council, with members like Mandela, Carter, the Dalai Lama and others who have experience of reconciliation. Each national government should have a Peace Department in place of a Defence Department ('security' and 'defence' are euphemisms for war). Each country should have peace academies, devoted to disseminating techniques for resolving conflict, in place of war academies. The first duty of these bodies must be to look critically at the motivations of their own governments before trying to intervene elsewhere. Western leaders' bombastic presumption that the violence of terrorism should be met by yet more violence is childish nonsense with horrific consequences.

Conflict is natural and can be a stimulus to creativity. The aim must be to understand the causes of conflict, to use conflict as a tool for growth, and to prevent it slipping into violence.

Violence leads to violence. But the cycle can be broken. An atrocity inevitably induces horror, then grief and then anger. Left to itself, the anger leads to hatred and revenge; further atrocities will then set the cycle of violence rolling faster.

Intervention can channel anger into seeking justice through law rather than retaliation. This is better, but still does little to prevent a repetition of the original atrocity.

Intervention can be taken further by analysing the causes of conflict with a view to removing them and bringing reconciliation. This requires a combination of determined, powerful leadership, imaginative action, and adhering resolutely to key principles. It is a process that can be studied and applied systematically. And it is economical. Nato countries spend 215,000 times more on 'defence' as on the main regional organisation devoted to conflict resolution (OSCE).

The Oxford Research Group has collected stories of many individuals, groups and organisations using techniques for alternatives to violence. In 1992, when militant Hindus destroyed the Babri mosque and violence spread throughout India, Lucknow avoided bloodshed because school pupils, following the teachings of Gandhi, got religious leaders to work together, and took to the streets in their thousands with loudspeakers appealing directly to the people to refrain from violence, carrying posters like 'The name of God is both Hindu and Muslim.' In El Salvador, some businessmen started a 'guns for goods' scheme, offering a $100 voucher for goods in local shops in return for each weapon turned in. By the end of the second week hundreds of weapons had been collected. They then called on the President for help, and in a short time 10,000 weapons were collected. In Belgrade in 1998 a few hundred students were trained in techniques of non-violent action. They in turn trained 20,000 election monitors, two for every polling station, so that when the elections eventually took place, it proved impossible for Milosevic to rig the results. Some incidents may seem insignificant in relation to global conflict, but politicians know how to make mountains out of molehills. Peace Direct, a new charity, aims to apply these techniques in the field.

There is a tendency to wait too long before intervention so that the use of hardware becomes inevitable. There are usually reliable signs of conflict: the right to vote, or to speak a language or to practice a religion may be threatened; theft or diversion of resources; occupation of territory; arms build-up; warlords making threats. If recognised early enough intervention can often be resolved through dialogue, mediation, bridge building, promotion of democracy, protection of human rights, support for indigenous dispute resolution, election monitoring, confidence building and restorative justice. These tools need to be more readily available than weapons. They are tools that can be studied and applied systematically. And, learning from the women of Wajir, they can be rushed to the site at the first signs of conflict.

Signs of hope: The British government recently allocated £110 million for conflict resolution, and there are 50 institutes in Britain studying small-scale non-violent intervention, such as at Sandhurst and Bradford Peace Studies

"Religious differences do not cause conflict. Religion comes in only once the lines of conflict have been drawn." *Zaki Badawi*

In a scientific conference a delegate held up a child-size talcum powder tin and explained that if this contained TCCD, used by the US in Vietnam, and was dropped into the water supply of a city the size of New York it could kill the entire population.

In 2002 the world spent $794 billion on armaments and $1 billion on war prevention.

"An eye for an eye leaves everyone blind."
Dr Martin Luther King

War Prevention Works
Dylan Matthews 2001

Inequality

a bequest from the 20th century

In spite of the benefits of modern technology we have entered a new century with **half the world living on less than $2 a day and seething with an overwhelming sense of injustice.**

A perverse global economy and trade framework has driven down commodity prices and has systematically transferred real wealth – crops, old growth timber and minerals – from poor countries to rich countries. In addition to this transfer of *real* wealth the poor are said to owe the rich piles of money as well – "if you don't pay up" say the rich "the global economy will crash." Poor countries, for some reason, sell their dwindling assets and cut spending on health, education and welfare in order to pay.

Four-fifths of the world's population now has to make do with only 14% of the world's wealth; the rest goes to support the living standards of the rich minority.

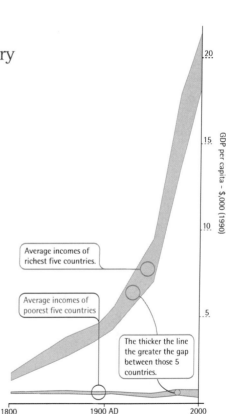

GDP per capita – $,000 (1990)

20

15

10

5

Average incomes of richest five countries.

Average incomes of poorest five countries

The thicker the line the greater the gap between those 5 countries.

1800   1900 AD   2000

Starting four centuries ago, Europeans believed it was their God-given mission to exploit and/or settle the rest of the world, taking resources and land from Americans, Africans, Indians, and Australians by force. Military colonisation is now frowned upon but economic inequality achieves the same results. The world's money is concentrated in just a few hands so that rich nations and corporations can buy politicians, buy scientists, buy media, manipulate public opinion, silence critical bodies, and destroy opposition within their own country or abroad. A tiny slice of their accumulated wealth is unimaginable riches to individuals or to an African village, town or even country. The use of tanks and depleted uranium to extract resources is now only necessary in exceptional circumstances.

And the wealth is not shared. The Human Poverty Index 1998 for industrial countries showed that the US, the wealthiest country the world has ever seen, had more people who were functionally illiterate (20.7%) than any other industrialised country, the highest proportion of population below the income poverty line (19.1%) and the greatest number of people who did not expect to reach the age of sixty (13%). Ten percent of the US population depended on private charity for food and 44 million had no health cover. The top 1% of households now has more wealth than the entire bottom 95%. In most countries inequality is rising as increased prosperity benefits only the rich élite, often leaving the poor even worse off.

There must be something structurally wrong with a world economic system that allows these inequalities to increase. Yet economists say that further economic growth will relieve poverty. And politicians claim that new initiatives on debt, aid and global trade can buck the imperatives of **an economic system that, by fundamental laws, transfers wealth from the poor to the rich.**

In the UK, 1% of the population had 20% of the nation's wealth in 1996 rising to 23% in 2001 (the fastest hike for the mega-rich since the War). The poorer half had only 7% in 1996 and that dropped to 5% in 2001. *Inland Revenue*

Boardroom greed
When UK shares fell 24%, boardroom directors (top 100 companies) rewarded themselves with a rise of 23%.

The world is not short of money. Growth is not essential. Redraw this graph - spread the wealth a bit - to double the income of the Chinese and Indians would hardly dent the income of the rich minority. "Redistribution - anathema! heresy! communism!" they cry, "The only way to help the poor is to keep the global economy growing." They say we must pile more and more income up that right-hand side, some will trickle down to the others. You can read this mantra every day in the business section of every newspaper. Read it often enough and you may come to believe it.

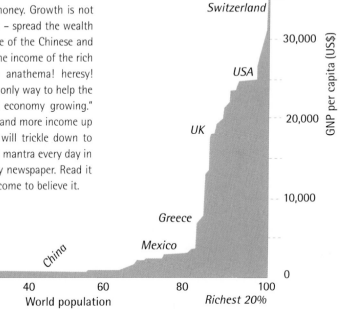

Distribution of the world's wealth

India 2004: stockmarket and GDP reached record highs. 'India shining' they crow. But Karnataka State returns showed record poverty: in Chamrajnagar district 93% of families now live below the poverty line. In other districts the figures are 88% and 77%.

Human Development Report
UNDP: annual

Usury & Greed

religious perversions

If you advance money to any
poor man amongst my people, you are
not to act like a moneylender; you must
not exact interest from him.
Exodus 22.25

Usury and greed used to be sins but now they are the twin towers of our economic life. Interest-on-debt, the modern phrase for usury, is how our economy works. Greed – encouragement of the desire for more, more and yet more – is the motor for economic activity.

From the Pentateuch onwards, Jewish and Christian writers condemned usury. The reason is obvious to anyone prepared to free her mind from platitudes about communism. Look at it like this. If you have spare money you can lend it to someone who desperately needs money. She has to work and pay back not only the money lent but some more as well; meanwhile you can watch your money grow and lend more to someone else. With interest, money flows from the poor person to the rich person, from the poor country to the rich country. So the first result of usury is that **interest is responsible for the constant growth of inequality.**

If the interest rate is 5%, every company that borrows has to be 5% bigger next year than this year or go bust. With compound interest it has to be twice as big in 14 years, four times the size in 28 years. The second result of an economy based on charging interest is that **global resources are consumed at an increasing rate.**

Consumption and economic growth are not exactly equal – a fat cat director can only stuff a certain amount of food and drink into his stomach – but economic growth requires a constant increase in the supply of resources. Each country is finite so cannot grow unless it loots other countries. Therefore the third result is that **an economy based on interest causes wars.**

The world is also finite so the global economy can't grow unless the resources of the world are looted. So the fourth result of usury is that **interest is destroying the planet**.

Leviticus sets out a benign economy where interest must not be charged, where debt would not accumulate but be cancelled at the Jubilee every fifty years, where those that fail must be supported, and where surplus is used for the purpose of allowing the land to rest and recuperate every seventh year.

But Christians ignore their scriptures. Usury and greed are so ingrained into western culture that we no longer question them. Value, which used to refer to the quality of social, artistic, intellectual and spiritual life, is measured only by money in the new dogma. The rich minority nations are forcing this pernicious belief-system on all countries and cultures throughout the world.

Not all cultures have the same values. Islam still does not allow interest to be charged on debt and one of the five pillars of Islam is *zacat*, the religious duty to distribute wealth to the poor. Islamists have good reason for their fundamental, often passionately held, objection to the imposition of usury and greed as a value system. Buddhists reject acquisitive values. For Hindus, business is just one of the four stages of life. In all religions value is measured by qualities other than money.

Indigenous cultures work on a cooperative approach. To them, wealth is the tribe, and individual windfalls are shared with anyone in need. Being a member of the tribe gives you security in your old age so there is no need to accumulate money or consume more than is necessary. These tribes have lasted tens of thousands of years without harm to their environment.

Culture and religion through centuries of civilisation explored many ways of understanding and defining the concept of value. Usury and greed were not among them.

Of all vile things current on earth,
none is so vile as money.
Antigone, Sophocles 441 BC

Economic Growth

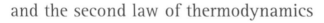

and the second law of thermodynamics

Frederick Soddy FRS (1877-1956) was a pioneer atomic scientist who received the Nobel Prize in 1921. He was deeply concerned about atomic power: "If the discovery were made tomorrow," he wrote in 1926, "there is not a nation that would not throw itself heart and soul into the task of applying it to war." The Royal Society ridiculed him for criticising new advances in science. He in turn criticised the Royal Society's comfortable view that scientists have no responsibility for the uses to which science is put.

Soddy considered that the economic system contained built-in elements for conflict and the destruction of Nature once science gave the power, so he applied scientific thought to economics. He was then ridiculed by economists.

Try this: A sack of grain is real and can be considered as wealth. But it reduces. It rots or is eaten by weevils and gradually turns to dust. That is the second law of thermodynamics. But if you talk about minus one sack of grain you are using a mathematical concept: it is virtual (i.e. conceptual) wealth, or debt, and it can grow *ad infinitum*. Soddy said that **the ruling passion of economists and politicians is to convert wealth that perishes into Virtual Wealth (debt) that continuously grows.**

So economists have turned the world on its head: you can store their money and it grows but if you store something real, like a coat, it decays and gradually loses value. They insist on making the real world of matter which decays conform to the purely mathematical concept of growth and compound interest. This is logical nonsense that can only lead to catastrophe in nature and the breakdown of society. To illustrate the absurdity of compound interest Soddy pointed out that if

Christ had invested £1 in our economic system it would now be worth £1,000 billion billion billion billion billion, or the world's weight in gold. He said in the 1920s that the result of this non-scientific thinking must inevitably lead to debt cancellation, revolution or war.

He referred to development since the Industrial Revolution as the flamboyant period of history, when humans are using up the capital stock of coal. This can only be a passing phase, after which we must live by sunshine – which has a maximum rate of flow. Therefore there is a limit to growth. Looking back after 75 years, has he been proved right?

Answer A

Economists might say: "He was an amateur who knew little about our discipline. There has been steady economic growth, wealth has multiplied and our standard of living has increased out of all recognition; our scientific achievements have been spectacular and the whole world is now open to markets, communication and tourism. Through our wealth we have gained the knowledge to deal with whatever problems of health and the environment that may arise. There are, admittedly, still pockets of need but the way to fill them is to ensure further economic growth." Is he saying that all our politicians, economists and businessmen are misguided?

Answer B

Soddy, if still alive, might reply: "Yes. The Wealth of Nature, real wealth, has been eroded. All our gadgets await the ravages of entropy. We have already passed the limit of growth and further economic growth may remove nature's life-support systems entirely. Individual problems with health and the environment will be swamped by general degradation. Virtual wealth, concentrated in a few private hands in only a small part of the world, has now reached levels that I could not have imagined and is leading to conflict and the breakdown of society. Economists have created a make-believe world that has nothing to do with the real world. To aim at yet further economic growth is suicidal."

Which is closer to the truth? Take your pick.

Beyond Growth
Herman Daly 1996

A Paradox

the history of growth: it makes things worse

Economic growth is a continuing obsession of our government, but a look at history indicates that, far from improving the well-being of all citizens, growth can often have the reverse effect. **The Index of Sustainable Economic Welfare (ISEW) shows a gradual reduction in the quality of life in the UK over the last 25 years** though the gross domestic product (GDP) has risen by 50 per cent. With GDP nations claim to prosper the worse they perform – the costs of disease, degradation and disasters are coupled with construction as positive contributions to GDP (true!). With ISEW they are negative. Richard Douthwaite analyses this paradox, devoting a chapter to each of the passages below: If you instinctively question these provocative statements, try reading his arguments in full.

🌿 Capitalism cannot survive without growth. Firms are compelled to expand to avoid collapse. In the world up to 1914, this compulsion built empires, destroyed indigenous cultures and, finally, led to world war.

🌿 Growth in Britain during the Agricultural and Industrial Revolutions made life progressively worse for ordinary people until about 1850. Conditions then began to improve – but as a result of depression, not growth. By 1914 living conditions might, just, have returned to their level of 200 years previously.

🌿 Major advances in the living conditions of the British people resulted from two world wars, the depressions of the 1920s and 30s and the freely redistributive policies of the 1945 Labour government. Whenever growth appeared, life for the majority got worse.

🌿 Because Mrs Thatcher sought to accelerate growth by improving investors' returns, her three governments engineered a major shift in the distribution of incomes and wealth in favour of the better-off.

- The growth process perverts the national economy within which it works. It causes unemployment and makes labour less affordable. It enables the concentration of economic power and requires ever-higher shares of the national income to be spent by the state.

- It was not until 1955 that accelerating the growth rate became the major British economic obsession. Since then, the methods used to generate higher levels of output have caused a large increase in chronic illness.

- All the indicators of the quality of life show that it deteriorated in Britain between 1955 and 1988. Unemployment, for example, soared and crime increased eightfold.

- Because their need for growth forces firms to adopt new technologies before their impact can be assessed, environmental disasters such as large-scale release of CFCs and PCBs are inevitable.

Douthwaite concludes that the only sustainable society is a stable society – history and logic show that there is no such thing as sustainable growth. It has been amusing to watch flat-earth economists desperately trying to match abstract patterns from the past with present stockmarket fluctuations, rather than looking at the systemic reasons for the failure of their growth paradigm.

Nature provides the model for a stable system. It has delightful and infinite variety; its complexity increases with time; when things go wrong it finds corrections or alternatives; it gradually turns dust into things of value; it captures pollution and lays it down into the earth's crust. But nature has no net growth. It is stable. It provides wonders on a finite planet.

To say that a stable no-growth economy is not possible simply shows the poverty of our imagination.

The Growth Illusion
Richard Douthwaite (1999 edition)

Making Money

it's really quite simple: deal in debt

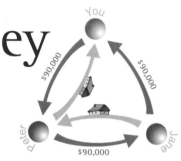

You start with £60,000 and call yourself a bank. You lend it to Peter who wants to buy a house. Peter buys the house from Jane, and Jane puts the £60,000 into your bank for safekeeping. You now hold £120,000 (£60k in cash plus £60k secured on a house).

You can now do the same with Michael and you hold £180,000 (the original £60k plus £120k in collateral). Soon you hold a million, most of it in collateral on houses on which you charge interest. You can now attract deposits at low interest to lend to others at high interest. Or you can invest your notional wealth and make money that way. With enough gall you could have started without even the original sum because they are only computer transactions anyway. **The more money you create by putting others into debt, the more interest you can charge.** The more debt, the more money and the more profit. This system only really took off with deregulation 20 years ago.

Governments make the notes and coins we use but these total less than 5% of the actual money in circulation. Banks and building societies have created the rest in the way described above as computer entries, not notes and coins. The money we use daily was created by private institutions, is owned by them and we pay them for using it, not once but year after year. Banks must maintain 10% 'capital adequacy' so they put aside that amount from net interest; it does not inhibit their ability to create yet more capital, it just puts up the cost of borrowing money and keeps them a nice little reserve.

Central Banks try to control the money supply by putting interest rates up or down. When they are down people borrow more and the money supply rises, then inflation threatens and interest rates go up – people lose their houses, and businesses go bust. This is a subtle form of torture that governments inflict on us.

Businesses now pay on average 28% of their income to service debt; the average house owners (two salaries) pay a fifth of theirs to service their mortgages. This leads to intense competition between companies to advertise and produce cheap, short-lived goods, and for consumers to struggle to remain in employment so that they can pay their mortgages. Western societies are aggressively competitive not because it is in our nature but because we must be to survive in a world where nearly half of all wealth is creamed off by the financial sector and the weak go to the wall. We have no choice.

If we work harder and the nation gets wealthier, will our indebtedness reduce? The sad fact is that the reverse happens. In Britain 20% of income services mortgages, the figure is 33% in wealthier US. In Japan generational mortgages, which extend liability to your children, have been introduced. No wonder the Americans and Japanese work all hours of the day. Stress is so great in Japan that 10,000 middle-aged men committed suicide in 1998.

"The modern banking system manufactures money out of nothing," said Lord Josiah Stamp, former director of the Bank of England, in 1937. "The process is perhaps the most astounding piece of sleight of hand that was ever invented."

US and UK credit and other 'promises to pay' reached ten times the level of real income (GDP) by mid 2003. Japan's economy crashed when this ratio reached nine in 1990.

"To say the financial system is crazy is an understatement. The situation defies description, and it beggars belief that no one involved in the operation takes a long hard look at what they are doing and just bursts out laughing at the innate insanity of the whole process."
Michael Rowbotham

The Grip of Death
Michael Rowbotham 1998

Banks

government, not banks, should issue money

Our money system gives banks a bonanza. Flat earth economists never question it. Government has abdicated control over it.

We admire Americans for their facility with money and commerce so it is surprising that the most damning criticism of the money system came from two of their most revered and intelligent presidents. Thomas Jefferson (1801-09) was alarmed at the development of the banking system. "If the American people ever allow the banks to control the issuance of their currency," he said, "they will deprive the people of all property. **I sincerely believe that the banking institutions having the power of money are more dangerous to liberty than standing armies.'**

Abraham Lincoln (1861-65) forged America into one nation. The two main causes of Civil War had been slavery and the financial stranglehold exerted by northern banks over plantations in southern states. Reconciliation was a truly great achievement. Had Lincoln lived longer he might have left an even greater legacy. He wrote a paper called 'Monetary Policy', a masterpiece of clarity and brevity. This is a key passage: "The government should not borrow capital at interest as a means of financing government work and public enterprise. The government should create, issue and circulate all the currency and credit needed to satisfy the spending power of the government and the buying power of consumers." **If the British government followed his advice instead of borrowing money from banks, it could spend an extra £46 billion on public services or reduce income tax by a third.**

Lincoln's policy would have led to the end of bank and money power in the US, and the world might have followed suit. But he was assassinated shortly after publishing this document and it was quietly suppressed

Jefferson and Lincoln's warnings have come true. In Britain the majority is deeply in debt to financial institutions that create money. But the assets of the few wealth-holders have spiralled upwards in value. In the majority world, poor countries have been enslaved by debt to banks, their economies destroyed and, because of their debt, corporations have been able to loot their assets and take over their essential services.

The amount of money in the world, created as debt, is now three times the value of goods and services available to be bought or sold. And **the main global commerce is currency speculation,** un-taxed, as $1,500 billion slosh backwards and forwards around the world daily.

Is inflation good or bad?
For people with debt (mortgages and credit cards) and dependent on wages or index-linked pensions, inflation in wages, food, clothes etc. is a good thing. The debt on their assets reduces in real terms. But the Bank's priority has been to protect asset values for the rich by reducing inflation and keeping interest rates low. With low interest rates people are tempted to go deeply into debt allowing the value of assets such as houses to rise. Low consumer costs and rising asset values are every wealth-holder's dream and every debtor's nightmare.

New Labour sold out to monetarism but did not like to take the blame for beggaring its voters so it handed control of the money system to the banks. The suffering, when the debt bubbles bursts, will be enormous.

Spread the risk! Collateral-debt-obligations – derivatives – you and I don't know what they're playing at. Actually nor do they. But the amount involved is four times the income of the world. When the music stops it will all come crashing down on our heads.

The Real Economic Outlook
NEF. ed. Ann Pettifor 2003

Interest-free Banking

and demurrage currencies

The JAK Bank in Sweden has over 20,000 customers and they don't pay or charge interest; they only pay administration charges.

The trick is in savings points. These are not just the amount of money in your account but also the time it is there, so savings points are measured as pound-months (krona-months in Sweden). Normally you can only borrow up to the number of pound-months that you have managed to save. But you can borrow up to eight times more if you continue to save while paying back the loan. The pound-months you save must match the pound-months you pay back; in this way you build up a nest-egg that cannot be withdrawn until the loan is paid off. **This balance of loans and savings insulates both the JAK bank and its customers from the crises of the money market.** You are not affected by the national interest rate.

The JAK movement started in Denmark in the 1920s and wherever JAK banks were established they increased prosperity in the area. Official banks took every opportunity to crush them because the JAK movement threatens the amazing concession society gives to banks to create money and cream off interest. At last the Swedish JAK bank has found a formula that is difficult for the establishment to stop. And it is spreading.

What about the bigger picture? – After all, this book has railed against interest. Bernard Lietaer, who has been described as the world's top currency trader, suggests that a currency, not just with zero interest, but with negative interest, is necessary and that it might be welcomed by big business.

Our interest-bearing currency forces companies into short-term investment: If you don't need a product till next year don't make it this year – money grows faster than inflation. Expenditure in 10 years costs a third at today's value. This is called discounted cash flow and is a technique used by all financial planners. If a company decides to be conscientious by investing for the future an asset-stripping predator will gobble it up. Currency growth leads to currency speculation, not to investment in real assets.

However, if a currency is constantly losing value, what is called a 'demurrage currency', the reverse applies. For example, if you are convinced that solar photovoltaics or fuel cells will have a big market in ten years' time, the sooner you build a factory the better. It will cost a lot more to do so after a few years because your money will have dropped in value. So a demurrage currency is good for business, it favours long term planning, it encourages people to maintain their property, and it cannot be used for gambling.

The money system used to serve the trading needs of big companies. But now less than five percent of trade relates to the real world of goods and services; the rest is currency speculation, growing at 15% a year and not even taxed! (The Tobin tax has been proposed but a demurrage currency would make this unnecessary). Countries, corporations and banks are helpless against this gambling. It requires instability otherwise there can be no profit in the game. Currency speculation is like an out-of-control cancer at the heart of our system. Not surprisingly, the big companies don't like trading with such unstable currencies so a quarter of world trade has already gone back to barter. Pepsi, for example, takes its profits from Russia as vodka; France builds nuclear power stations in exchange for oil. This return to barter is surely an admission of defeat for flat earth economists and it is time they started thinking about mechanisms that serve the real world.

Demurrage currencies have served prosperous civilisations well in the past – the Ming dynasty, ancient Egypt, 10th to 13th-century Europe (the age of cathedrals) – and it is now quite possible that companies will turn to the stability of a demurrage currency to escape the merry-go-round of the speculators.

The Future of Money
Bernard Lietaer 2001

Wörgl

money that is not worth keeping

Have you ever wondered at the beauty of buildings from the 12th and 13th centuries in southern Europe, when about 600 new towns were built with solid stone houses that have survived to this day? Ironically, it was not a politically stable period. The wars waged by the Church on the Cathars necessitated much reconstruction. The wars were partly about religion and partly about the Church's loss of revenue.

Inadvertently a rather strange system of money was responsible for the reconstruction that gives us such pleasure today.

In the Holy Roman Empire rulers of the dozens of small independent states issued thin silver coins called *bracteates* which would be reclaimed at three quarters of their value when the ruler died. Realising that this was rather a good idea the rulers soon started reclaiming and reissuing them more frequently. So holding on to money was risky – it was no store of value; **better to use it while you had it to build houses with lasting value.** This led to a high demand for construction labour so wages were good, working hours were short (about six hours a day) and there were at least 90 religious holidays a year. It greatly improved the quality of life and was wonderful for the local economy.

But when gold coins were introduced in the fifteenth century it became worth storing money instead of using it because of the amount of precious metal it contained. You could keep it under your mattress. So demand for labour dropped, wages fell, unemployment appeared, many businesses closed down because people could earn more by lending the money they had accumulated on interest rather than by trading. And, to cap it all, rulers had to find other means of taxation.

The idea of issuing money that is not worth storing has cropped up frequently since. Wörgl, a small town in Austria, was suffering from the Depression in the 1930s. There was 35% unemployment and local taxes were seriously in arrears, crippling the work of the council. The mayor negotiated a loan from a credit union bank and printed scrip notes. These were guaranteed against the national currency though you only got 98% of their value if you exchanged them. You had to stamp each note monthly to one percent of its value, so it cost you to keep it and you used it as quickly as possible. Half the council's staff wages were paid in the scrip and the mayor also allowed local taxes to be paid in scrip, so businesses and shops were prepared to accept it. The effect was to stimulate local trade, tax arrears were paid off and there was full employment. The council was able to employ 50 extra people, paying their wages entirely in scrip, to repair and surface streets, and to extend the sewerage system. Then they built a ski jump and a reservoir without incurring any debt. The scrip notes circulated around the local economy so there was little call on the inflating national currency. Not surprisingly, other towns started to copy the scheme. The Central Bank, alarmed that it was losing control of the money system, took out legal proceedings and closed it down soon after it started.

Many similar schemes were started in the United States with the same response from banks. In March 1933 President Roosevelt forbade any further scrip issues being advised that the financial system was being taken out of the government's hands – by the people!

economic activity using a local currency

Short Circuit
Richard Douthwaite 1996

Global Eco-Currency

four currencies

Anyone who takes part in a baby-sitting circle uses an alternative currency, it may be IOU chits, entries in a diary or just a mental note; there is nothing odd about multiple currencies. It is very odd, however, to use just one currency for speculating on the international money market, buying cabbages, and saving for your old age. Richard Douthwaite suggests four currency systems each designed for a specific purpose:

- ⑧ an *international currency* for trading between nations;
- ⑧ a *national-exchange currency* for trading within a nation,
- ⑧ various *user-controlled currencies,* and
- ⑧ a *store-of-value currency* for your savings.

The *international currency*, would be an emissions-backed-currency-unit, an 'ebcu', and take its value from the right to emit greenhouse gases (see Contraction & Convergence). There is no international currency at present: various national ones such as the dollar, the pound sterling, the yen and the Swiss Franc are used instead. **As these are debt-based and not linked to anything real, the global economy is extremely unstable.**

To get the new currency going, the IMF would issue each country with 'ebcus' based on its 1990 population. No more would ever be issued. A nation's existing wealth would remain in its other currencies. Then, each month, the IMF would issue coupons called Special Emission Rights (SERs) to each country on the same population basis. These coupons would confer the right to emit greenhouse gas and would be handed in whenever fossil fuel was purchased. Each year, the number of SERs issued to each country would fall so that, within a few decades, the total amount of greenhouse gas the world released would match the earth's capacity to absorb it.

National governments would decide how many of their SER coupons to distribute internally to all its citizens and how many to trade internationally. India, which uses little energy at present, would have surplus SERs to sell. The US would use all its coupons internally and need to purchase more on the international market using its 'ebcus' in payment.

The *national-exchange currency* would be used for buying and selling within a country but not as a store for one's long-term savings. If trade increased the central bank would print more of this currency and spend it into circulation, thus reducing the government's tax needs. This might cause mild inflation but this is fine because it induces you to use money before it loses value, thus encouraging trade and employment.

The national-exchange currency would be supplemented by a wide range of *user-controlled currencies* such as Local Exchange Trading Schemes (LETS), scrip issues, Time Dollars and systems modelled on the Swiss Wirtschaftsring.

The *store-of-value currency* would be a fixed quantity of a special form of money used only for purchasing and selling capital assets. If more houses or shares were traded, for example, the need for this currency, and hence its value, would rise in relation to the national-exchange currency. So:

- 💲 The *international-currency* would keep the world economy within the carrying capacity of the planet.

- 💲 The *national-exchange currency* and many *user-controlled currencies* would encourage economic activity within a nation.

- 💲 The *store-of-value currency* would link your savings to the prosperity of the country – no more and no less.

Other thinkers suggest incremental change. But, with the likelihood of a global crash, it might be better to adopt Douthwaite's radical proposals than to try and patch up our present perverse financial system.

The Ecology of Money
Richard Douthwaite 1999

Citizens' Income

for a civilised civilisation

*"The time has come for us to civilise
ourselves by the total, direct and
immediate abolition of poverty."*
Martin Luther King

The idea of a Citizens' Income was pioneered by Henry George in the 1930s but was overshadowed by the introduction of the welfare state. It is now coming into its own. In Europe it is being championed by BIEN, Basic Income Network Europe. In New Zealand it is called the Universal Income. In South Africa it is the Basic Income Grant. In Canada, the Guaranteed Annual Income. In the US, the Citizens' Dividend.

A Citizens' Income would be the right of every woman and man in the country, equally. It is not pay, welfare or charity. It is her or his dividend of the nation's inherited wealth. Attempts to alleviate poverty up till now have been indirect and often demeaning – welfare, housing, education – why not abolish poverty itself. The change would be dramatic. It would do away with the iniquitous benefits trap and it would give purchasing power to millions that at present have none. There would be an explosion of local economic activity and the crippling stress of modern life would be removed.

Can it be afforded? Clive Lord shows that a Citizens' Income (CI) of £74 per week (£97 for 60+) would require a net increase in income tax of 7% but **all taxpayers with an income of less than £30,000 would be better off**. This figure is low but note two other proposals. The Domestic Tradable Quota (p40) would increase the CI for the frugal carbon-user. And if government, not private banks, issued money (p70) the CI could be doubled. It would greatly simplify the bureaucracy of benefits and tax returns. Some researchers suggest that a nation's 'commons' and its inherited wealth – enhanced land value, the airwaves, and wealth that is not part of the market economy – should be distrib-uted as a calculated, not an arbitrary, figure.

It sounds too good to be true, but Alaska already runs a citizens' dividend by distributing royalties from oil companies to all its citizens, equally; this is only about $1,200 a year, $4,800 for a family of four, but it has boosted local economies, reduced child poverty and, though small, it demonstrates the principle of a Citizens' Income.

Look at the bigger picture. Our civilisation is wealthier than any previous civilisation. Who created this wealth? Not the corporate fat cats. It was built up by farmers, industrialists and the work and imagination of countless individuals over many generations. It is an inheritance from which all should benefit.

It would profoundly change the basis of our economy and so is difficult to imagine. But could anyone have seriously imagined, or wanted, the world we are actually creating? A world in which just 220 people own more than the joint wealth of half the world's population. The wealth of these few people doubled in just four years and soon the entire planet, humanity's inheritance, built up over centuries, will become the private property of a few individuals. The rest live in fear of loosing a job, of not being able to pay a mortgage, of falling ill, of penury in old age. People are driven to vicious competition or theft to gain illusive security. A billion people round the world live in fear of starvation. We have achieved a world of hatred, terrorism and cut-throat competition that drives businesses to expand regardless of sweatshops and environmental destruction. **A better world is possible.**

no worries!

A Citizens' Income would free people to improve their lives. It would provide them with a financial platform from which they can choose the life they want to lead. It would give them the ability to demand proper wages and conditions. They could get out of work they find unsatisfying making way for others that want the job. They could avoid work that harms the environment. Small-scale farmers could survive. Local shops

Why don't they abolish poverty?

within a community would again become viable. The trend that at present centralises all economic activity would be reversed, making it possible to curb the tyranny of corporations. Small-scale employers would benefit because of lower staff costs, as they would only need to top up their CI and could employ more staff. There would be no need to produce unnecessary or short-lived products in order to generate employment. People would not have the compulsion to amass excessive wealth for their old age or to pass to their children.

Unearned income has always benefited some in society – those with inherited wealth or whose partners have high salaries. A Citizen's Income would extend this benefit in a small way to others who do not share their advantage. This is a less divisive route to social justice than calling for revolution. It would remove the plight of those who have no option but to beg. Most would want to earn more than the Citizens' Income but some might choose to bring up a child or write a book while being content with a low income. A Citizen's Income would do more than anything else to give us a humane and civilised society.

The BIG idea

Unemployment among South Africans runs at almost 50% so that means-tested welfare payments, if attempted, would be too expensive to administer with any pretence at fairness and would encourage corruption. The World Bank and IMF forced the government to impose 'structural adjustments' that deprived the poor of health and social provision but did nothing to stimulate the economy.

Something new is at last giving hope. The South African government is considering the BIG idea, the Basic Income Grant. This grant would be given to all citizens and it would be clawed back through tax from people with an income. A BIG coalition has been formed of labour unions, church bodies, NGOs and organisations like the SA New Economics Foundation. All eyes are now turned on South Africa to pioneer this new people-centred economic idea.

A Citizens' Income
Clive Lord 2003

Vibrant Cities

creators of prosperity

Back in 1950 Taiwan had a rural economy with low wages that attracted companies from America. These factories provided some employment but did little to stimulate a local economy. Taiwan might have remained a backward supply region like so many poor countries today.

It was not global free markets or aid that changed things; it was its government. It distributed land to peasants and, crucially, attached strings to landlords: they had to invest part of their compensation in local light industry. The government also used training grants, tariffs, quotas and export subsidies to protect the emerging industries. People learnt skills from the US firms, they were subcontractors, they replaced imports with locally made goods, they invented new products and they financed their new businesses with the local money from former landowners. The city of T'aipei and its region became a hive of activity operating first locally, then trading in the Pacific Rim with cities at the same state of development, then globally.

A 'supply region', whether it produces minerals, food or oil, benefits only as long as someone is prepared to pay good money for its produce. During this period it may be wealthy enough to import all the gadgets it needs for a diverse and prosperous lifestyle and does not need to make these things itself. But, when other countries no longer need its goods or when they can drive the price down, it can no longer afford imports and cannot make them itself. It slips back into poverty. However if, during the prosperous period, it replaces imports with locally made goods and focuses its economic activity in cities, it can build an economy that retains prosperity.

What has produced strong city regions in the past? Ports had a natural advantage when ships were the main international transport. Cities near coal mines prospered until oil and electricity arrived. Some cities, like Seattle, still benefit from military contracts. European cities developed economic strength because each had its own currency that would fluctuate to encourage exports or allow imports depending on the business cycle. Tariffs enabled America to break its dependence on Europe.

Tariffs, import quotas and protection against takeover by foreign investment are essential tools for poor countries. And a network of city regions at a similar stage of development, with fluctuating currencies, is their best environment. **Above all, they must avoid simply selling basic commodities for other countries to manufacture, or agricultural produce for others to process;** they should manufacture their own frying pans, computers and pencils, not sell crops to earn money to buy these things from rich countries. These regions are referred to as 'import replacement economies' because their vitality arises from replacing imports with increasingly sophisticated local products. Rural areas need to be part of one of these vital regions in order to get adequate value for their more basic produce.

In the West, cities no longer have their own currencies; it is now national currencies that fluctuate. These fluctuations are determined by the needs of a dominant city region, so London flourishes while the north of Britain declines. The Italian currency suited Milan but not the south. Each Scandinavian country, however small, retains one viable city region, but only one. The Netherlands, sensibly, has grouped its cities into the Ring City as a single entity. Singapore, T'aipei and Hong Kong each has its own currency, which partly explains the spectacular success of the Pacific Rim. The single European currency will result in just one city region becoming dominant while outlying areas decline – unemployment in Portugal and East Germany is already rising. America is a special case because the inflow of goods in exchange for the use of the dollar across the world has prevented the trade deficit detracting from its internal prosperity.

Indians have a genius for improvisation and import replacement. The country's future may depend on being able to resist the pressures of a global economy that aims to make its rural areas, once again, simply supply regions for a western empire. India has a sixth of the world's population with a market large enough for a full diversity of internal trading. Trade with Europe and the US should be limited to high value goods where the value added has been made within its own borders. India's great city regions are widely separated; each could adopt a separate currency and, by trading with each other using fluctuating exchange rates, develop self-reliance and sophistication. Like the Pacific Rim.

Patents

The single global patent regime prevents the spread of knowledge and hence the ability of poor countries to add value. India's 1970 law rejecting certain western patents enabled it to replace imports with local production; and its cheap generic medicines have saved millions. It was only worldwide protest that allowed South Africa to use affordable drugs from India to treat Aids (a recent agreement will once again prevent this). Corporations fear loss of income for research, but their R&D budget is tiny compared with the money they spend on marketing. And only a tenth of the R&D budget goes on drugs relating to 90% of global disease, the bulk being spent on rich-country afflictions like obesity.

Cities and the Wealth of Nations
Jane Jacobs 1984

Mosques & Churches

misunderstandings abound

A group of building workers line up. One stands in front to lead the prayers. Draw a line around this group, put a bulge at the centre of the side facing Makkah and you have the plan of a mosque.

From the noisy, chaotic activity of a bustling covered *suq* in Damascus pass through a small door into a large calm colonnaded court where groups of men and women sit on carpets in the shade and talk, read or sleep. Mosques are enclosures for the community and fill for prayers five times a day. Churches have different qualities. In gothic cathedrals holy rites are performed at the altar and the architecture soars towards heaven. Orthodox churches embody mysteries shrouded in incense. Protestant churches, chapels and assemblies encourage the congregation to focus on a preacher.

Muhammad had been both prophet and head of the community and there was no separation between religion and state. The *Qur'an*, revealed to him over a period of 23 years, insists that a Muslim's first duty is to create a just, egalitarian society, where poor and vulnerable people should be treated with respect.

There are five 'pillars of Islam.' First, a Muslim is required to make a brief declaration of the unity of God. The other four – prayer, zakat, ramadan and al-hajj – emphasise social equity and community. All should pray five times a day as a communal act that is done, not just thought or said. Zakat, almsgiving as a proportion of income, should encourage the fair distribution of wealth in the community; many Muslims see western values of competition and self-interest as being a direct threat to the kind of society to which they aspire. The ramadan fast is a vivid reminder of privations suffered by the poor. For the fifth pillar, al-hajj, pilgrims wear a uniform white garment that allows no difference of rank or standing.

With its care for the community, Islam appeals to the poor. The Muslim is a social being in the body of Islam, the *ummah,* that transcends nationality. When a Muslim nation is ravaged, the hurt and shame is felt universally and by each individually.

Muhammad did not believe that he was creating a new religion but was bringing the primordial religion of humanity to his Arabian tribe. God had sent messengers to every people on the earth to tell them how to live. When they disregarded these basic laws, creating tyrannical societies that oppress the weak and refuse to share their wealth fairly, their civilisations have collapsed. This required *jihad* ('struggle') for right living. Seventh century Arabia was a country of warring clans which may explain some harsh phrases in the *Qur'an,* but they are always followed by injunctions like "if they let you be, and do not make war on you, and offer you peace, God does not allow you to harm them." War is only permissible in self-defence and is always evil.

Southern Spain was, for hundreds of years, a Muslim country that preserved civilisation in Europe and embraced thriving Christian and Jewish communities. In 1492, Ferdinand and Isabella made their first conquest. Moslems and Jews were forcibly converted, massacred or expelled and many Jews fled to the Ottoman Empire where they were welcomed. Western histories gloss over the barbarities of the Christian invasions and crusades. But the tables turned. Western modernism eventually won and the Ottoman Empire collapsed.

Just as the West's consumerism and weapons of mass destruction do not sit easily with the Sermon on the Mount, al-Qa'eda's terrorism does not sit easily with Islam. But the social and egalitarian aspects of Islam's five pillars may help us to understand why it is the fastest growing religion in the world.

 In Santarém, Portugal, the mosque, after 700 years of disuse, is being restored along with the synagogue and the monastery of Sao Francisco. Might they again experience the intellectual and cultural dynamism that was once there?

The Battle for God
Karen Armstrong 2001

Basic Needs

isn't everyone as happy as we are?

Helena Norberg-Hodge worked in Ladakh, in the Himalayas, one of the harshest climates in the world, scorched by the sun in summer and frozen for eight months of the year. She noted the immense care taken over the use of minimal resources, relying on the outside world only for salt and tea – there was literally no waste. Ladakhis worked hard in the summer but at their own rate, accompanied by laughter and song; the distinction between work and play was fluid. Winter was a time for festivals, parties and story-telling. They understood their own needs – and these did not relate to western style development.

After visiting this poorest of countries for 16 years she said, "Their sense of joy seems so firmly anchored within them that circumstances cannot change it. At first I couldn't believe that the Ladakhis could be as happy as they appeared. It took a long time to accept that the smiles I saw were real." Is this 'noble savage' romanticism or do we need to be more precise in defining human needs?

Manfred Max-Neef, a specialist in human-scale development, identifies nine basic needs:
- 😊 **Subsistence** – *creation, health, food, shelter skills, work, feedback*
- 😊 **Protection** – *security, society*
- 😊 **Affection** – *friendship, family, love*
- 😊 **Understanding** – *curiosity, education*
- 😊 **Participation** – *responsibilities, interaction, community*
- 😊 **Leisure** – *play, fantasy, intimacy, privacy*
- 😊 **Creation** – *skills, work, feedback*
- 😊 **Identity** – *belonging, groups, recognition*
- 😊 **Freedom** – *autonomy, rights, dissent*

But basic human needs can be satisfied in very different ways by different cultures. If we propose to make changes to the economic system of a country we should check how the changes are likely to affect any one of these nine basic needs. To facilitate this he discusses each need against four aspects of living – what we are – what we have – what we do – how we interact.

Severe deprivation in one need may paralyse all other considerations. This is particularly the case with hunger (subsistence) that paralyses 13% of the world population. But the same is true of other needs. Social exclusion (participation) in an affluent society may lead to criminal behaviour. Total lack of affection or loss of identity may lead even wealthy people to suicide.

For politicians and bureaucrats the concept of basic human needs is usually limited to food, health and education – to be met through aid and advice handed down from international agencies. They see only the economic goods that represent a fraction of real need and are surprised when imposing these solutions, with the best intentions, causes havoc in countries with a strong spiritual and traditional culture.

For Max-Neef human-scale development comes from the grass roots. An economic strategy may satisfy one need and not another. If it causes extreme deprivation to any one of the needs it must be abandoned however beneficial it appears to be in other respects. Development will be destructive unless those involved participate fully in deciding what their real needs are and how they might be satisfied.

Back to Ladakh: globalisation may bring additional income but the influx of money and consumer perishables may simply make them aware of the deprivations of an extreme climate while destroying a culture that in the past has satisfied all their fundamental human needs.

In 1995 it rained in Ladakh for the first time in living memory. Their houses are built for a dry climate. Climate change? They have done nothing to deserve this.

From the Outside Looking In
Max-Neef 1992

'Them' or 'Us'

a Gandhian approach

Henry VIII is usually credited with creating Britain's centralised state, a system that Thomas Jefferson later struggled to reject in the New World. Everything now flows from central government. Gandhi also suggested precisely the opposite and various projects in India are applying his principle: that **the local community, at grass-roots level, should be the basic unit of government.**

Seventy-five villages at Lathur, in South India, have been identified as being below the poverty line and in need of aid. But it is the village (100 to 300 people), not the authority, which decides which individuals are in need and how the aid should be distributed. The village council of 20 men and 20 women is elected annually and the post of headperson rotates.

Mr Rajamani could double his income if his well

were deeper. He applied to the village council. The village council assessed his proposal and approved the necessary loan (from the authority). He repaid the loan plus interest to the village council, not to the authority. This is the route by which aid flows to the village community.

Ninety-eight percent of loans are satisfactorily repaid and the failures are usually for a particular reason that can be understood by the village council. So the community builds up a fund. Once the fund reaches a certain size the authority withdraws and the village itself continues with the process using its own accumulated funds. After five years, 35 of the villages no longer require further aid. A community bank, controlled by the village councils, handles the funds.

It is necessary, of course, to ensure that each village keeps to the system and is not bullied by a few individuals or taken over by a political group. This is done, not by the authority, but at an annual two-day gathering of all the villages. In addition to the business in hand this gathering becomes a festival, a place of contact and even a marriage market. It is the lowest tier of the state electoral system that Gandhi recommended, where each tier takes responsibility for its own affairs and aims to determine the policy of higher tiers of authority. The higher authority must be the servant of the lower. In other words, the villager is the maker of his/her own destiny, and is his/her own legislator, through his/her chosen representative. The ultimate storehouse of his/her power, should other means fail, is non-violent civil disobedience.

In Britain, even more than in the US, power is now held by a clique at the top subject only to occasional elections – a system we call democracy, though a political analyst would call it 'elective oligarchy', rule by a small group of people. Each tier distrusts the one below, so rules and regulations abound. The lowest tier controls thousands. Local authorities are reluctant to allow a street community to decide how its road might be allocated between children and cars, or to approve the design of new buildings; to set up its own arrangements for repairs, or re-cycling of waste and water, or to combine with adjacent communities to provide its own school or clinic. A street community in Hull secretly grassed its road overnight for the Jubilee in 1977 and had it ripped up by the authority the following week. It took 20 years for the community to get it back to grass through official channels. Citizens only really feel involved when they themselves make the decisions that vitally affect them. There is a fundamental difference between decisions made by 'US' and decisions made by 'THEM'.

It is no wonder that social exclusion has become a major issue in Britain. When people cannot determine their own destiny the community falls apart. The vital step is from mere consultation to the exercise of citizen power through participation. This requires the management of budgets by communities that are small enough for all to be involved – street-scale communities. This is democracy.

Reclaim the Streets

Two old cars collided. Each driver shouted, took an axe from his boot and hacked the other car. Traffic gridlocked. Onlookers cheered. That's how the first street party started in 1995. On another occasion 3,000 danced to the tune of 'What a Wonderful World'. Trees were planted in a six-lane highway under the hoop skirts of clowns on scaffolding. The largest party drew 20,000 in central London. Then it went international with a Global Street Party in 1998 on the day that G8 leaders met. In Prague police action provoked violence. In Sydney, Australia, police helped and joined in the fun.

Email helped. People converged, as if from nowhere. The number of bicycles suddenly multiplied, "We're not blocking traffic," the Critical Mass riders said, "we are the traffic." People made their own fun without asking the authority's permission or relying on any corporate largess. The urge for entertainment, through acts of civil disobedience, became festivals. The streets, for a brief day, become commons.

The realisation had dawned that our streets had been colonised by the authorities, by cars and by commerce – just as France had been colonised during WW2. It was time to tell the authorities and big business, the streets belong to us not to you.

"Freedom is to be attained by educating the people to a sense of their capacity to regulate and control authority."
Mohandas Gandhi

Fences and Windows
Naomi Klein 2002

Wealth in Poverty

a tribal's view

Wealth means different things to different people. For tribal people, money has little meaning. It is community that they value.

The community at Gudalur, South India, is extremely poor. They used to live in the forest but could not prove ownership of any land. In their culture there was no conception that land *could* be owned. **Land, water and air are regarded as commons, available for all to use.**

The government sold the forests in which the tribal community *'adivasis'* lived. It was assumed that the forests were empty and Brooke Bond acquired large tracts as tea plantations. Tribals continued to live on the edges. But how could they secure their rights? The only way was to plant permanent crops. But when they did so the forest rangers pulled up the crops and destroyed their homes.

In 1984 Stan and Mari Thekaekara, social activists, persuaded five of these tribes, totalling 2,000 families, to act together. When individuals were threatened, the community gathered to protest. They secured land for some, but ownership of individual plots did not help the community.

The *adivasis* decided that the only way to strengthen the community was to obtain a tea plantation. They prepared a business plan and, with Stan's help, obtained a loan to buy it. The plantation is now their own. In two years the yield doubled, and it supports a school and a hospital. From being virtual outcasts, the *adivasis* are now respected. Their tea fetched high prices because of its quality but, rather than dividing the profits among the group working on the plantation, the pickers themselves said that any extra earnings should go to the community. **They said that if they became wealthy while others remained poor, their community would fall apart.**

Mari said: "The *adivasis* were clear about their wealth. It is our community, our children, our unity, our culture and the forest. Money was not mentioned. We, the *non-adivasis*, were stunned. As we discussed concepts of poverty further, we realised that they didn't see themselves as poor. They saw themselves as people without money."

Stan and Mari visited the poor Easterhouse estate in Glasgow as part of a North-South exchange and the question of poverty again forced itself upon them. In Glasgow everyone had a television, running water, heating and benefit payments. The *adivasis* would regard these things as inconceivable luxuries.

"But most of the men in Easterhouse hadn't had a job in 20 years," Mari said, "They were dispirited, depressed, often alcoholic. Their self-esteem had gone. Emotionally and mentally they were far worse off than the poor at Gudalur, though the physical trappings of poverty were less stark."

Stan and Mari brought a group of *adivasis* to Germany. The gift they valued most from their hosts was being treated as equals – something they did not experience at home. But they were speechless when they saw an old people's home. "How can children send their old parents to live alone? We must ensure that such things never happen in our society, no matter how much we progress." Then Karl, their German host, came home one evening preoccupied with the news that he might lose his job. Bomman, an adivasi, worried all night for his new German friend. "I have an idea," he announced in the morning, "I can make bamboo flutes when I go home and Karl can sell them here till he finds a job." Through contacts like these the *adivasis* now trade directly with their friends in Europe.

When a group was next threatened with eviction, it was the contact with their friends in Germany that persuaded Brooke Bond to concede – confrontation might damage their image internationally. The *adivasis* had found that community, with its ability to empower, even when up against a trans-national company, could be extended across the world.

Is this just a story about a remote community or does it touch on human values deeper and more lasting than those of global capitalism?

🌱 Free trade can hurt. A letter received from Ramdas in Gudaur in July 2000 said, "One of the most unfortunate issues has been the drop in price of both tea and coffee. The government has opened up the Indian market and large imports are being allowed. This has created a fall in the price for producers while the price in shops remains the same."

🌱 Kariyan, of the Kattunayakan tribe in south India, made a clearing in the jungle and planted ginger. As luck would have it the price for ginger shot up last year from Rs60 to Rs160 and he made money. Now he has none left. When people asked him for money, he gave, without asking questions. Does he need lessons in money management? Kariyan values the tribe. He shares what he has with others and vice-versa. He did not calculate. He acted as he, and they, had always acted. If he had gone off on his own, the money would have run out eventually and he would be destitute. He has security as long as the tribe has security, which means as long as they all act instinctively as he did.

Kattunayakanis do not need to store money for their old age, they do not consume more than they need, they do not cause harm to the forest or its animals because they have a strong sense of interdependence with their surroundings. Instinctively. The Kattunayakan tribe has facial features resembling Australian aborigines, and anthropologists confirm the connection. The startling deduction is that the tribe has had continuity from the time when humans migrated to Australia 50,000 years ago. They have a sustainable way of living.

"There is no quiet place in the white man's cities. What is there to life if a man cannot hear the lonely cry of the whippoowill or the arguments of the frogs around the pond at night?"
Chief Seattle

Odious Debt

a humane American idea

It appears that international law has one rule for the strong and another for the weak.

The concept known as 'odious debt' was established by the US in 1898. America had invaded Cuba but found that their new colony had large debts to Spanish banks. The US refused to pay these debts, arguing that the debts had been "imposed upon the people of Cuba without their consent and by force of arms." Thus the doctrine that neither the people of a country nor its new government is responsible for the odious debts of a previous regime was established. However, do you imagine that in recent years poor nations were allowed to invoke this doctrine? Certainly not!

South African apartheid was defined by the United Nations as a crime against humanity. When Nelson Mandela became president, he and the people of South Africa inherited more than $18 billion in debts. Surely no debts could be described as more odious. But the IMF warned that unless the debts were repaid, however odious, South Africa would be isolated by the international community. Money that should have been used to build schools and homes, to create jobs and to repair the environment, instead was sent to the US, UK and Swiss banks that had financed apartheid.

Mobuto, dictator of Zaire, was a friend of the North and the North lent him money. He was known as the 'kleptocrat' because of his lavish palaces and purchases from Europe. When he died in 1998 he left debts of $13 billion. Zaire is now the Democratic Republic of Congo and the West wants its money back. The new government should be spending every penny on rebuilding the shattered country. Instead, every man, woman and child in the country must repay $260 in debt.

Investors lent the Philippines' Marcos regime the money to build the Bataan nuclear power station, and Westinghouse channelled millions of dollars through Swiss banks to secure the contract. It was in an earthquake zone so was never used. The Marcos' personal wealth was $10 billion but it is the Philippine government that must pay the debt.

Debt gives world institutions power to enforce policies that benefit trade. Through the imposition of 'structural adjustments', the IMF and World Bank have effectively controlled Tanzania's economy since 1985. In the following 15 years Tanzania's GDP dropped from $309 to $210 per capita, literacy fell and the rate of abject poverty rose to over half the population. The World Bank complained "One legacy of socialism is that most people continue to believe the State has a fundamental role in promoting development and providing social services."

Poor countries must pay their debts, however odious. But Long Term Capital Management, a US-based hedge fund, was treated with concerned sympathy when it landed itself in debt. The Federal Reserve immediately found $3.6 billion to bail out its friend.

Dealing with the Asian crisis, the IMF declared, "Reducing expectation of bailouts must be the first step in restructuring Asia's financial markets." Asian companies were bankrupted and became rich pickings for western companies. However the IMF ultimately agreed $120 billion funds to be made available to pay Asian debts to – whom? To western banks, of course. Taxpayers money was used to to reimburse private banks that had lent rashly and western companies took over Asian businesses at knock down rates.

The guiding principle for the IMF and the World Bank is this: whatever happens, whoever is at fault, the wealth of western creditors must be protected and enhanced.

Take the Hit
New Internationalist May 1999

Third World Debt

view of the rich

"The notion that for the Jubileum someone can come along and forgive that debt is whimsical. If you have a society based on debt forgiveness, who's going toinvest in debt anymore? So you really screw up the market."
Mr. Wolfensohn, World Bank President

Poor nations owe the rich a lot of money. $200 billion is owed by 41 Heavily Indebted Poor Countries (HIPCs).

The First World, say the rich, gave aid and loans in order to help the Third World develop its economies and to combat poverty and disease. In addition the World Bank has been providing health, education and agricultural advisers. The Agrichemical Revolution, pioneered by First World scientists, greatly increased productivity since the 1950s and helped poor countries adopt modern techniques to replace traditional farming methods. Much of the aid was squandered by corrupt regimes and many countries mishandled their economies. With this perspective, the First World argues that it has made serious efforts to help poor countries rise out of poverty.

If a bank lends to a corrupt or chaotic company that then goes bust the bank loses its money and must write off the debt. But the First World knowingly lends to countries that cannot possibly pay back the capital let alone the interest. It also lends to corrupt regimes for political reasons. The debts are calculated in hard currency, usually dollars, so they increase in real terms as the local currency devalues. On top of this the debts attract compound interest. But the North never writes off bad debts – they accumulate.

So the total Third World debt is many times the amount actually lent.

Don't feel sorry for rich countries that have lost money. This is a deliberate calculated policy. It puts poor countries in their power. Debt enables the International Monetary Fund (IMF) to impose *structural adjustments* that require debtor countries to open their markets. This in turn has forced down wages. The resulting collapse of commodity prices has increased profits for western corporations but reduced income to countries without a manufacturing base.

Nicaragua's health budget is a quarter of the amount it spends on servicing debt. Mali repays more than it spends on health and one in four of its children die before the age of five. Zambia's repayments are greater than its spending on health and education. Debt repayments cripple struggling economies and cause hunger, disease and death. If a dictator had imposed the policies of the IMF he would be found guilty of genocide. Many people in poor countries regard the IMF as a terrorist organisation, responsible for more death and misery than al-Qa'eda.

By contrast, the financial assets of northern banks have been growing at the rate of $2,500 billion a year – more than the third world debt.

At a meeting in Cologne in June 1999 the G8 made a gesture to the HIPCs, promising to reduce their debt by $100bn. Campaigners were jubilant and there was dancing in the streets. They had forgotten that the IMF and the World Bank were involved. Five years later only eight of the 42 HIPCs have received the relief promised. In the few instances where debt has been cancelled, spending on health and education has more than doubled.

The First World has, however, put its head into a noose. If a man owes a bank $10 thousand the bank has him in its power. If he owes it $10 billion he has the bank in his power. **The Third World owes $2,500 billion and has the global economy in its power.**

At the WTO meeting in Cancún in September 2003 the majority nations had their first experience of the power behind collective action. They can either bring the global economy crashing down, noting that after 55 years it has failed to produced an equitable world, so why persist? **Or they can demand debt cancellation and a new world order based on environmental survival and social justice.** Let's help them to choose the latter.

Poor countries are losing $700 billion in earnings annually due to the trade barriers of industrial countries, according to Renato Ruggiero, former director of the WTO.

Annual expenditure on health per capita: US $2,765, Tanzania $4, Ethiopia $2.

In July 2002 over three million people faced starvation in Malawi. The World Bank and IMF had forced Malawi to sell 28,000 tons of maize to repay dollar debts.

Anti-IMF and World Bank protests occurred in 25 countries in 2002, with 111 separate incidents of civil unrest.

Debt repayments by the Third World are nine times the aid it receives.

June 2002
£24bn wiped off stockmarket in one day.
£21bn committed to bring railtrack back into public ownership.
$3.8bn fraud by WorldCom
£1bn G8 *conditional* aid to Africa.

Ecuador's debt repayments amount to nearly a third of her budget, twice the budget for social welfare. Nearly two-thirds of Ecuador's population live in poverty.

"IMF rescue packages are intended only to rescue western creditors."
Ellen Frank, Professor of Economics, Boston

Between 1503 and 1660, 185 thousand kilos of gold and 16 million kilos of silver were transferred from Central America to Europe. One would hesitate to accuse Europe of looting or stealing; it was surely a loan. If Central American nations only ask for modest interest, perhaps half of what we are charging them, the debt we now owe them would have 300 digits.

But why don't poor countries just refuse to repay unfair debts?

"Only when the last tree has died and the last river been poisoned and the last fish been caught will we realise that we cannot eat money."
a First Nation American

The Silent Takeover
Noreena Hertz 2001

First World Debt

view of the poor

Money is not the only form of wealth. Would you envy a billionaire his money if he were locked in a prison cell? If we can't enjoy the world around us we are indeed poor. So there are two kinds of wealth: your money and your environment. There are also two kinds of debt – the money you owe and the damage you have done to the environment.

The First World says it is owed lots of money. And not in devalued rupee, baht or rouble but in hard western dollars, so the original debt may now be multiplied by five or 10 times due to devaluation and compound interest.

The Third World has a very different view about debt. It is saying the word 'third' is an insult from people with myopic minds set on money. "We have qualities of culture, spirituality, heritage, traditions, festivals, cuisine and language quite as good as yours (and our children are not obese).

"Who has been using up the earth's fossil fuel, mineral and timber resources?

"Who has been polluting the atmosphere with greenhouse gases and causing hurricanes and rising sea levels to devastate our countries?

"Who has been profiting from the chemicals that have got into our food chain, degraded our soil and poisoned our aquifers?

"Who has been over-fishing the oceans and depriving us of our offshore fisheries?

"How dare the 'Money-First World' require us to make 'structural adjustments' to our economies when it makes no structural adjustment to the social harm and environmental damage it is causing throughout the world?"

It says the First World has a massive debt to other nations for depleting the natural capital of the world, but this debt is fundamentally different from Third World Debt. Financial capital claimed by the First World is artificial; it is a human invention that is meant to conform to rules largely invented by the Money-First World. Natural capital, on the other hand, is real and finite. It is the fossil resource fixed in the earth's crust through millions of years of photosynthesis; it is the constant daily flow of energy from the sun; it is the ability of the atmosphere to keep the earth pleasant and habitable.

The majority nations could have a case in law against the rich. To take just one example, pollution by industrialised nations has led to climate instability – causing drought and famine in the Horn of Africa, flooding in Venezuela, Bangladesh, Orissa and Mozambique, sinking island states and much more – the industrialised nations should compensate. You can quantify loss of infrastructure but how do you quantify loss of life, loss of livelihood, loss of culture? The Money-First World has been responsible for a sustained holocaust in the Third World.

The UN World Disasters Report 2000 calculated that the First World debt was $13,000 billion to the Third World. Add to this the poverty and deaths caused by a perverse global economy and unfair trade practices. Add to this the deprivation and deaths caused by environmental damage. But calculations have an air of fantasy.

Law is the rich nations' approach to resolving conflict. But applying systems of legal justice in these circumstances will simply lead to endless conflict while the world slips into catastrophe. Many money-poor nations have a different system of resolving conflict: look for common ground. The poor want a world economy that is fair. The rich need environmental stability. The rich minority nations must humbly ask the majority nations to share the damage they have caused. The money-poor nations are asking for confrontation to be put behind us and – please – stop thinking of everything in terms of money and military bully-power. We must work together to save the world from environmental catastrophe and we must eradicate hunger.

The Post-Corporate World
David Korten 1999

Free Trade

comparative advantage for corporations

Tatu Museyni cultivates coffee in Tanzania. The price she gets for coffee has halved over the 20-year period since 1980. It halved again in the last two years. Her income is now down to $40 for the whole year. Her children no longer have education and the family face starvation. Worse is in store. Researchers in Hawaii have developed GM coffee plants whose beans all ripen at the same time making it possible to pick by machine. When machines replace pickers, Tatu Museyni and 25 million others may have no income at all. On the other side of the planet, Nestlé boasts in its annual report, **"Thanks to favourable commodity prices profits have reached a record high."**

The price of other commodities also dropped between 1980 and 1997: sugar down 73%, cocoa down 58%, rubber down 52%, rice down 51%, cotton down 36%, copper down 30%. And prices have continued to drop. The reason is obvious. A corporation will move its operation to where it can get coffee cheapest, say Brazil. If India drops its price, it will move there. If Brazil drops its price further, it will move back there. It is a race to the bottom. This is free trade, otherwise known as market fundamentalism or corporate capitalism.

Consider a company that buys land from farmers in Kenya to grow flowers for sale in England. Previously self-respecting farmers become dependent labourers, and land that once fed the rural community now provides luxuries for the rich. But then the company may suddenly transfer its operations to Uganda if labour is cheaper there. Rich countries get cheap luxuries; the company makes a good profit, GDP in the Africa rises and their business élite benefits. But, in Africa, the poor become even poorer and, in England, flower-growers lose their business.

Three-quarters of all international trade is now in the hands of multinational corporations, enabling them to drive down the cost of commodities, to have more customers and to locate their facilities where environmental and labour standards are low. They dismiss horrific living and working conditions and early death as 'commercial reality'.

Corporate free trade is forever associated with the *laissez-faire* monetarist policies of President Reagan and Margaret Thatcher, and now of New Labour. John Maynard Keynes had a more enlightened and humane approach: "I sympathise with those who would minimise entanglement between nations. Ideas, knowledge, art, hospitality, travel – these are the things that should of their nature be international. But **let goods be homespun whenever reasonably possible and, above all, let finance be primarily national."**

Corporate free trade over the last 30 years has been a period of increasing poverty and social disintegration, alienation, violent insurgency groups, breakdown of democracy, environmental degradation and new diseases. A third of the world will soon be living in city slums and more people are hungry than ever before.

I think we had more freedom before

For the global élite, free trade corporate capitalism is a fundamentalist religion, impervious to reason, evidence, or compassion. Like communism before it. The religion has a central dogma that an 'invisible hand' will somehow result in the poor benefiting from the excessive wealth of the rich. World leaders should open their eyes to the ghastly results of their fanaticism but all they can offer is, "Hold tight, it will be all right in the end'" This was Stalin's story. In the end, the oppressive regime collapses, leaving social and financial chaos.

There is support for free trade among businessmen and governments in poor countries. The World Bank's data showed that free trade raised their GDP. To demonstrate this it commissioned research. But to its distress the report, 'The Simultaneous Evolution of Growth and Inequality', showed that free trade benefits only the élite in poor countries but sinks the lower 40% into deeper poverty. These findings did not support the fundamentalist beliefs of the Bank's hierarchy and so were deleted. The editor of the World Development Report, professor Ravi Kanbur, resigned in disgust.

Market fundamentalism in action

In the last two years 500 export factories in Mexico have closed, sacking 218,000 workers. Their $1.26 an hour wage was too high. Alcoa now produces auto parts for the US in Nicaragua where workers get 40 cents an hour. Now these workers have been told to work for even less or the jobs will go to China where workers will get 16 cents an hour, work 16 hours a day, 7 days a week with no health insurance and no pension.

When global players, like Asda-Wal-Mart, drive down prices, those at the bottom have no option but to enter rich countries illegal-ly where they can be exploited, like the 20 cockle pickers drowned in Morecombe Bay.

Value added

The US and Europe promote their own produce with subsidies, export credits and tariffs and prevent others using their knowledge by enforcing patents. Poor countries are forced, with sanctions and withdrawal of aid, to open their markets. This prevents them adding value within their borders and locks them into poverty.

Comparative advantage

Two countries trade hats and oranges. One is good at making hats; the other grows oranges. A country benefits from selling what it grows or makes better or more cheaply than other countries. This theory of 'comparative advantage' is taught to economics students as the underlying principle of trade and is trotted out by economists and politicians as one of the benefits of the free trade religion. It made sense when Adam Smith formulated the theory in the 18th century but it has been turned on its head. Now that capital and investment are mobile, the rich buy up any profitable land or business in poor countries. With global corporate free trade, a poor country loses its only advantage.

The law of comparative advantage now means: "multinational corporations benefit by taking over those things that a country grows or makes better or more cheaply than other countries."

Hungry for Trade
John Madeley 2000

Just Change

linking consumer and producer

If the global trading system is not serving the poor, can the poor change it?

An organisation of adivasis, tribal people, in south India is doing just that. They had bought a tea plantation when greenleaf tea fetched Rs40 for 4kg. Free trade policies then forced the price down relentlessly so that by 2004 they only get Rs12/4kg (plus Rs4 for transport). While India's economy booms, tea pickers – like most other primary producers, those at the bottom of the chain – are suffering desperate and increasing poverty. So what is their strategy?

'Greenleaf' are the leaves picked from bushes. It takes 4kg of greenleaf to produce 1kg of made tea. It costs the factory Rs20 to process the tea. Traders now buy made tea from the factory for Rs36/kg and shops sell it in towns after packaging for Rs160/kg (Rs450/kg in Britain).

The *adivasis* have an inbuilt attitude that people should be able to get what they need (a strange and deviant idea to market fundamentalists). They say that tea is one of the essentials of life and should not be treated as a commodity for making profits off each other. Everyone drinks tea. With the present system, the poorest in society are using a large proportion of their earnings on essentials that support a trade system that, in turn, drives down their earnings. Madness. There must be many groups like themselves, they reasoned, that drink tea, and that grow lentils or make textiles for clothes – all essentials. They contacted some of these groups. They also contacted womens' groups. And they devised a scheme, calling it Just Change.

Instead of selling greenleaf tea to the factory, they agreed to *buy* an equivalent amount of made tea from the factory at an enhanced price of Rs60/kg (not Rs36/kg at which the factory is selling to others). The factory undertook to pay the pickers Rs40/4kg greenleaf, thus retaining its mark-up and having a guaranteed sale. With normal trade the pickers lose control of their product when it goes to the factory. With Just Change the pickers receive a proper wage and retain ownership of the product. They then distribute the made tea to the groups they have contacted at very much less than the price these groups would buy from shops. The groups drink what they need themselves and market the rest to local teashops.

would be totally alien to the adivasi life-view. When profit is achieved they use it wherever there is greatest need. The first episode was when they sent a lorry load of tea to a group of latrine workers who drank some and sold the rest to local teashops; this produced a profit and the two groups met to discuss how it should be used. The adivasis were so horrified by the conditions forced on the latrine workers that they insisted the latter keep all the profit. Other profits have gone to setting up a school and a hospital. Just Change aims to meet the necessities of life and to build communities.

Once this is in place the other groups do the same in return so that all receive a proper wage for the work they do in production and all have access to necessities at below the market price. In addition, work is generated for the womens' groups to package and sell tea, lentils and clothes to shops in their areas.

Might this develop into just another parallel trading system for the pursuit of profit? This

"The challenge for us today is to create a radically new structure, which will directly link consumer and producer communities and measure the economy not just by the profits generated but by how equitably this profit has been distributed."
Stan Thekaekara 2003

stan@gudalur.com

The WTO

a better way is possible

"I do not believe that a country with 4.5% of the world's people can maintain its standard of living if we don't have more customers."
President Clinton 2000

Regulation is necessary, otherwise the strong will exploit the global commons at the expense of the weak. Trade regulation started with the General Agreement on Tariffs and Trade (GATT) in 1948.

The WTO grew out of the GATT but things have gone badly wrong. After 56 years there is widespread degradation and depletion of resources. Half the world's population lives on less than $2 a day, half of those on less than $1. In rich as well as poor countries farmers are committing suicide because trade rules have destroyed their livelihood.

The WTO has been hijacked by corporate interests and its purpose is now to promote trade. Period.

There is no higher authority, and corporate free trade, 'market fundamentalism', has become the governing principle of the world. The WTO – deliberately – now ensures that the weak cannot protect themselves against the strong, and the strong are not restrained from over-exploiting the global commons.

The WTO aims to weaken national government. A strong government in a poor country might discourage the export of raw commodities or crops so that value can be added to them within its own borders. It might also exclude imports that had been cheapened unfairly by subsidies in the exporting country. These are both ways in which the poor could climb out of poverty. But they are forbidden.

Under WTO rules governments are not allowed to favour local firms, prevent foreigners having a controlling interest in local companies, favour trade partners or subsidise domestic industry, (though it has not prevented massive US and EU subsidies to their farmers and exporters). Governments are not allowed to interfere in a market to pursue social objectives such as racial, ethnic or gender equality, nor to favour friendly countries that might have special needs. The rules work to the advantage of corporations which benefit from economies of scale, which can undercut to capture a market, which are immune to local consumer feed-back and which can shift their production at short notice to countries with lower wages and fewer environmental or labour regulations. In all these fields manufacturers, suppliers, retailers and farmers in poor countries are at a disadvantage. It is hardly believable but the WTO sets maximum, not minimum, standards for environmental protection.

Trade spreads films, music, language, business methods and attitudes. **The WTO is therefore establishing of a single culture, globally.** But modern communications also make everyone aware of stark and growing inequality, disintegrating societies, collapsed economies, violent reaction from disaffected groups and environmental crises.

The WTO claims to arrive at decisions by consensus. The Quad (Canada, EU, Japan and the US) sets the agenda and detailed wording of its decisions are hammered out in Green Room meetings to which awkward delegates are excluded or forcibly ejected. Green Room decisions are then presented as 'consensus' and binding on all. Objectors are often neutralised by phone calls from heads of state to the delegate's government (George Bush made fifteen such calls during the Cancún meeting). So formal disputes have largely been limited to differences among the rich.

For the notorious WTO meeting in Seattle in 1999 the chair was the head of the US delegation and delegates from poor countries were sidelined and ignored both in the preparations and during the conference. At the following Doha meeting, Europe and the US undertook to reduce subsidies and both reneged on their promises. **Subsequent meetings were held in remote locations behind police barriers, vividly demonstrating that the WTO had lost legitimacy.**

By September 2003 the majority nations had had enough. The EU was responsible for the collapse of the Cancún talks by refusing to withdraw new issues. The US had anyway decided to deal bilaterally – "WTO or no WTO we plan to do just what suits us" said one US ambassador – indicating that it would continue to use the old imperial tool of 'divide and rule.'

But the majority nations demonstrated at Cancún that by working together they can take control. Either the WTO will be made democratic or a new body will be set up with population-based majority voting.

The primary trade objective of a world organisation should be to encourage and enable the poor to add value to their commodities and crops within their own communities and boundaries. Countries with poor communities must be encouraged to use appropriate subsidies, tariffs and import quotas, but these restrictive measures should be reduced on a **sliding scale** as their economies strengthen. Rich countries should remove all fiscal measures that promote exports or benefit well established companies, but not those measures that help small businesses and growers to serve a local market.

This policy was pioneered by the American Founders in their struggle against the tyranny of British companies and led to Alexander Hamilton's 'infant industry protection' policy that regulated US trade from 1789.

TRIPs
(Trade Related Intellectual Property Rights)
The TRIPs agreement protects patent rights – almost all of which belong to western companies – and countries are no longer allowed to make patent regulations to suit domestic conditions. The TRIPs agreement is a restriction on trade in favour of corporations, a blatant infringement of the WTO's own free trade agenda. It limits the use and development of knowledge, paralyses scientific research, benefits only the rich, prevents technology-transfer to the poor, denies affordable access to life-saving medicines, appropriates farmers' use of traditional knowledge, reduces bio-diversity and allows the properties of plants and animals to become private property.

The Age of Consent
George Monbiot 2003

The GATS

exit democracy and peace

Negotiations for the General Agreement on Trade in Services (GATS) should be abandoned until an independent assessment has been made.

The GATS came into being in 1995 following pressure from multinational corporations (MNCs), but details are still being worked out. The European Commission admits: "the GATS is first and foremost an instrument for the benefit of business." There has been widespread protest in poor countries as they see their services taken over by foreign companies but, after nine years, the WTO has carried out no independent research into its effects.

The rich say that many poor countries have not been able to afford adequate investment in their service sectors so multinational corporations will help them with both capital and expertise – the rose-tinted view of privatisation.

Under the GATS, national governments must submit to certain rules when handing over services for privatisation. Countries are free to decide which sectors they will subject to GATS rules though the aim is for all to be privatised in the end. **The GATS enables corporations to invest, acquire land and take over essential services in any country that signs up.**

Health, education, electricity, water, sanitation, post, telecommunications, transport, banks, investment, insurance, radio, television, film, rubbish collection, setting up of retail stores, construction, tourism, land – they all fall within the orbit of the GATS. The preamble to the GATS has many statements to reassure its critics. But the preamble is not legally binding. The rest of the document is legally binding and it specifies that governments must not regulate in any ways that are a hindrance to trade. Even a government's right to hold back essential services is being eroded in current discussions. Article V1.4, the 'Necessity Test', makes the GATS Dispute Panel arbiter with veto powers over whether a government's regulations conflict with free trade imperatives. Bureaucrats that meet in secret determine what a government can or can't do. National parliaments are thus demoted to mere advisory bodies within their own countries.

Many consider the GATS to be the most evil and dangerous of all interventions by the WTO in the affairs of poor countries. If politicians have lost power over economic measures they are left with only the manipulation of prejudice to catch votes.

The Quad listened to delegates from poor countries but the GATS magicians kept vital cards up their sleeves:

- **Trick 1**
  The process is irreversible. If a government or a dictator has privatised a service and listed it to the GATS, such as railways, health or water, a subsequent democratically elected government cannot take it out.

- **Trick 2**
  The regulation of trade is enforced by sanctions. Sanctions by poor nations are a scarcely noticed pinprick for the rich. Sanctions and withdrawal of assistance by rich nations can destroy the poor.

- **Trick 3**
  Only rich-nation businesses benefit. One cannot conceive of companies from poor countries bidding for health, education or water services in the US or France or the UK.

- **Trick 4**
  A country is not free to encourage its own expertise and indigenous culture by, for example, limiting the number of foreign citizens working as architects.

- **Trick 5**
  Awkward negotiators from poor countries are withdrawn following a phone call to their governments from a powerful country.

- **Trick 6**
  A poor country may be persuaded to bargain away a particular service because it needs to retain, say, favourable tariffs on textiles.

- **Trick 7**
  It is virtually impossible for indigenous companies to compete with MNCs.

- **Trick 8**

  A country may not realise what it is letting itself in for. Having listed tourism, for example, it may not be able to limit the number of hotels provided by foreign companies at an historic site.

- **Trick 9**

  Negotiators from poor countries are frequently excluded from critical meetings.

- **Trick 10**

  Countries cannot insist on foreign firms working jointly with domestic firms, or that a proportion of shareholders be domestic, or that some assets be held to cover liability for damages.

The General Agreement on Trade in Services signals the end of national government. When investment is open to all comers, when financial services are run by global banks, when local trade cannot be given preference, when the local language and culture cannot be protected, when governments are forced to sell essential services to multinational corporations, when even the land of a poor country can be appropriated by the rich – what is left? **Exit democracy.**

Britain privatised its railways, the French did not – enough said!

GATS for violence and starvation

Democracy brought an end to famines in India in 1947. The new government gave priority to livelihoods, food security, land distribution and it imposed a ceiling on land ownership. But in 2002 famine returned to six states in spite of overflowing grain stores. Why? The World Bank had forced India to dismantle its humanitarian structures in favour of free trade policies. Without democratic influence over economic content, politicians can now only bid for votes on the basis of prejudice, fear and hate. Communal violence, cross-border aggression and starvation returned.

The IMF is un-democratic and its proceedings are as opaque as crude oil.

- World population: **India:** 17% US: 4.3%
- Share of votes: **India:** 1.9% US: 18%

Wealth-based voting was rejected by the American Founders and was abolished in Britain in 1832.

Argentina

Argentina, like Haiti, implemented World Bank and IMF policies fully during the 1990s. The peso was linked to the dollar. Everything from oil to water was privatised.

At the first sign of economic trouble the global companies transferred their loot abroad. Wealthy individuals who saw what was happening also hastily converted their pesos to dollars. Citizens lost jobs, savings, dignity and many now scour refuse heaps for half-eaten bread. One of the world's richest countries joined the the poorest in a matter of days. Argentina shows what lies in store for countries that adopt the IMF's neo-liberal agenda. Its government is begging for loans. It should be demanding reparations.

The US is the world's biggest exporter of cotton. Its farmers receive $4bn subsidies for producing $3bn-worth of cotton. Its cheap cotton exports are bankrupting growers in poor countries.

FTAA (Free Trade Area of the Americas)

This proposal will enable corporations to compete for publicly funded services currently provided by governments, from healthcare and education to social security, culture and environmental protection. There have been protests throughout the Americas at this threat to democracy. In September 2002, ten million people from nearly 4,000 municipalities throughout Brazil responded to the question "should the Brazilian government sign the FTAA treaty?" A resounding 98% said 'NO!' But US power ignores democracy.

"Our objective with the FTAA is to guarantee control for North American businesses over a territory which stretches from the Arctic to the Antarctic – free access over the entire hemisphere, without any difficulty or obstacle, for our products, services, technology and capital."
Colin Powell. Secretary of State

The Best Democracy Money Can Buy
Greg Palast 2002

Water Denied

crimes against humanity

Control of water-distribution in a water-stressed country is effectively control of a populace. Denying water rights to the poor is a crime against humanity.

Water is more essential than oil. Bottled water is more expensive than petrol. So, as water becomes scarce, excitement among corporations and their CEOs is palpable. Companies are building massive pipelines, giant sealed water bags and supertankers to transport water to those that can pay high prices. Western governments are bullying poor nations to surrender their water to the GATS. The World Bank wants grandiose water schemes and says that the private sector must be involved. **But any child can work out that 'the market' prefers to serve the rich rather than the poor.**

We all have a right to water, particularly to the rain that falls on our community. But water is being stolen. The examples below are just a drop in the ocean.

The World Bank pressurised the Bolivian Government to privatise water companies, and a subsidiary of the US giant Bechtel gained a 40-year concession. The poor faced water-rate increases of $20 a month (the minimum wage is $100 a month). Even collecting rainwater in rooftop tanks became illegal without a permit. In La Cochabamba, streets were barricaded, 30,000 protesters seized the central square and police fired on the crowd, which then swelled to 80,000. Bechtel left the country. A coalition of people's activists has taken over the water company (impossible if the GATS rules had already been in force). A few days later Wolfensohn, Director of the World Bank, had learnt nothing from the experience, claiming that Bolivia still needed "a proper system of charging," and that there was no option but to pay international prices for a valuable resource. But the fight is not over. Bechtel is suing the Bolivian government and the government is harassing the coalition of activists. Eventually, because of his IMF policies over natural gas, the president was harassed out of the country.

✠ In India a local tribe had always used water from an artificial *tanka* in the forest but it could not prove ownership. The government sold the *tanka* to Pepsi who fenced it and kept the tribe out. Pepsi even tried to prevent the tribe storing rainwater from their roofs.

✠ South Korea is using virtually all its available water. A detailed World Bank study predicted that withdrawals for industry and housing will increase and water for agriculture will decline from 13 to 7 billion tons by 2025.

✠ Taxpayers are helping the state of Orissa in India to privatise water distribution through an ill-conceived aid project. Water rates have increased tenfold. Millions will be forced to migrate into city slums. But thousands of small farmers are taking control of the water services through non-violent direct action.

✠ A subsidiary of the French company Générale des Eaux was granted a 30-year contract to deliver water in a rural province of Argentina. Water rates doubled and the water turned brown. Customers forced the company out of the province by refusing to pay their bills.

✠ In another incident in Argentina a water company behaved properly. It subsidised poor areas by charging wealthier customers a 'solidarity tax'. The wealthier customers used the courts to get the surcharge ruled illegal. Under the GATS, it is impossible for a company to pursue socially desirable policies.

✠ In 1995, water privatisation in Puerto Rico left poor people without water while US military bases and tourist resorts remained well supplied.

✠ When companies fail to milk the poor they pull out. Suez abandoned Manila. Saur left Mozambique. Vivendi is moving out of all poor countries. The poor are left to rebuild the ruins.

Coke and Pepsi have 80% of the soft drink market in India. Their bottles contain 30 times the toxic pesticides like lindane and DDT allowed in Europe. A Coca-Cola plant in Kerala dug borewells. Farmers' wells dried up and the little left was unfit to drink; many had to walk five miles for the nearest clean water; crops failed and employment crashed. The company's waste was distributed as fertiliser but after three years it was found to contain toxic metals including cadmium that causes kidney failure and lead which is dangerous for pregnant women. The local council withdrew Coke's licence to operate and farmers trashed its offices. The government banned Coke and Pepsi from its canteens.

Almost all parts of India have adequate rainfall if the water can be stored where it falls and/or fed into aquifers. 'Rainwater harvesting' is the most efficient water conservation and distribution system. Thousands of *tanka* reservoirs throughout the sub-continent testify to this tradition. Communities consider they have a right to the rain that falls on their fields. But the WTO has re-defined water as a 'need' not a 'right' and a 'need' can be bought and sold – to corporations.

Abhorrent policies result when money takes precedence over civilised values. Lawrence Summers, when chief economist to the World Bank, noted that health-impairing and death-inducing pollution costs are lower in poor countries. "I think," he wrote "the economic logic behind dumping a load of toxic waste in the lowest-wage countries is impeccable and we should face up to that." 80% of US electronic waste is sent to Asia. 100,000 Chinese villagers are paid $1.50 a day to salvage valuable parts and dump the rest, unaware of the chemical hazards. Much of it goes into irrigation canals and from them into the food chain and aquifers.

In cities, participatory water management has proved a viable alternative both to privatisation and to traditional bureaucratic public models. **"Through social control, democracy and transparency, people push us to be more efficient,"** says Carlos Todeschini of Porto Alegre, Brazil.

www.corporateeurope.org

The First MNC

little has changed

The East India Company was the first major shareholder-owned multinational company (MNC). It found India rich and left it poor.

When the company was established in 1600, and for 150 years thereafter, there was nothing England could export that the East wanted to buy. Spices, textiles and luxury goods sailed west. Only money sailed east. **It was the ability to acquire land and control government services that made the fortunes of the Company – and broke India.**

As the mighty and opulent Mughal Empire declined, the Company acquired land beyond its vulnerable trading ports, extorted taxes, manipulated terms of trade in its favour, and built up a private army. In 1757 Robert Clive fought and defeated the Nawab of Bengal. Later, Lord Cornwallis defeated Tipu Sultan in the south. In both cases, and in many lesser incidents, the Company's executive officers extorted huge ransoms and accumulated unimaginable wealth. This wealth was obtained, not so much from its fashionable society customers back in England, as from suppliers in India, from defeated rulers and from taxes imposed on the populace. India financed its own impoverishment.

Under the Mughals, taxes had been collected through a complex pattern of mutual obligation. This was too complex for the Company. At a stroke the *zamindars*, tax farmers under the Mughals, were transformed into landlords, and Bengal's 20 million smallholders were deprived of all hereditary rights. Just five years after the Company secured control of Bengal in 1765, revenues from the land tax had tripled, beggaring the people. The devastating effects last to this day. These conditions turned one of Bengal's periodic droughts, in 1769, into a full-blown famine. An estimated 10 million people died. But, rather than organise relief efforts the Company actually increased tax collection during the famine. Granaries were locked, and grain was seized by force from the peasants and sold at inflated prices in the cities.

The Company became feared for the brutal enforcements of its monopoly interests. For example, it would cut off the thumbs of weavers found selling cloth to other traders to prevent them ever working again. In rural areas two-thirds of a peasant's income was taken in tax, nearly double that under the Mughals. The Company's performance, through pursuing profit for its shareholders and its chiefs, contrasted starkly with its claim, in the mid-19th century, that it ruled for the moral and material betterment of India. The British government followed the Company's policy. To maintain a monopoly in salt, the rulers made it illegal for Indians to make their own, and consumption of salt was forced even below the minimum prescribed in English jails. This disgraceful control of an essential commodity was only withdrawn after Gandhi's famous Salt March in 1930.

In Britain, so powerful was the Company that attempts to control its affairs could bring down a government. An attempt, led by Edmund Burke, to place the Company's Indian possessions under Parliamentary rule led to the dismissal of the government. The general election that followed was so generously funded by the Company that it secured a compliant parliament – a tenth of the seats were held by 'nabobs'.

Booty from India created this new class of 'nabobs', the chief executive officers (CEOs) of Georgian England. The nabobs themselves had no conscience about their wealth. Robert Clive, having extorted a fortune after the battle of Plassey, defended himself at a House of Commons enquiry into suspected corruption, saying that he was 'astounded' at his own moderation at not taking more. Only a few dissenting voices, like the Quaker, William Tuke, pointed to the humanitarian disaster that the Company had wrought in India. But the case for reform was overwhelming and in 1784 the India Act transferred executive management to a Board of Control, answerable to Parliament – a kind of public-private partnership.

Although the Company pretended to a mission to make Indians 'useful and happy subjects' the underlying ethics of the public-private partnership remained the same. By the 1850s, just £15,000 was being spent on non-English schools – the military budget was £5 million. Railways were built to speed access of British goods to Indian markets. Mill-made cloth brought from Britain shattered the local village economies, which were based on the integration of agriculture and spinning. The great textile cities of Bengal collapsed. The Governor-General reported, "The misery hardly finds parallel in the history of commerce. The bones of the cotton weavers are bleaching the plains of India."

Indians were worn down by the British dominance, by the unfair trading rules, the crippling taxes, the draining of India's wealth and the contempt in which the majority was held. Retaliation was inevitable. The final insult was forcing sepoys to use a rifle cartridge greased with cow and/or pig fat – an outrage to both Hindus and Muslims. Catastrophe struck in 1857. The British could not understand the hatred and called it 'mutiny'. The massacre of Europeans generated a ferocious bloodlust in English society and led to brutal reprisals. Long-standing plans for increased dominance in all spectrums of Indian life and economy had at last received their justification. In 1858 the East India Company was abolished and direct rule by Queen and Parliament was introduced.

Corporate exploitation followed by an outrage led to Empire. Is history repeating itself?

Loot: Resurgence 210
Nick Robins 2002

Ending Tyranny

the struggle of the American Founders

*"I believe in this beautiful country. I have
studied its roots and gloried in the wisdom
of its magnificent Constitution. I have
marvelled at the wisdom of its founders and
framers. Generation after generation of
Americans has understood the lofty ideals
that underlie our great republic.
I have been inspired by the story of their
sacrifice and their strength.
But today, I weep for my country."*
Senator Robert Byrd, March 2003

Boston's citizens threw $15,000 worth of tea into
the harbour. That was a lot of money in 1773 –
and a lot of tea. The tea belonged to the East
India Company, the world's first multinational
corporation (MNC). The British government then
decreed that the harbour would be closed until
the people of Boston reimbursed the Company.
That led to war and rejection of the tyrannical
regulations imposed by a remote government on
behalf of a corporation. Poor countries today
have similar feelings about remote government.

The American Founders were determined to
prevent tyranny enslaving the New World,
whether the tyranny of an aristocracy or of
standing armies. But it was trade dominance that
aroused their greatest passions. At the time,
virtually all members of the British parliament
were stockholders with the East India Company,
a tenth had made their fortunes through
the Company, and the Company funded
parliamentary elections generously. British
traders and politicians prospered through the
activities of this first MNC that was sucking
wealth from around the world. The parallel with
today's corporate and political life in the United
States is remarkable.

Measures were introduced in the New World to
prevent corporate tyranny. Corporations received

their charters from individual states and these were for a limited period, say 20 or 30 years, not in perpetuity. They were only allowed to deal in one commodity, they could not hold stock in other corporations, their property holdings were limited to what was necessary for their business, their headquarters had to be located in the state of their principle business, monopolies had their charges regulated by the state, and all corporate documents were open to the legislature. Any direct or indirect political contribution was treated as a criminal offense. Corporations had their charters removed if the state considered their activities harmed its people.

Railroad companies had traditionally been referred to as 'artificial persons' and when the Fourteenth Amendment gave all 'persons' equality before the law they desperately tried to claim that equal rights applied not just to slaves but to them as well. For eighteen years the Supreme Court consistently ruled that corporations did not have the rights of human persons. Then the *Santa Clara County vs. Southern Pacific Railroad* legal case reversed this. Corporate tyranny in the US and throughout the world can be traced to this one case.

Textbooks only quote the headnote of this case, not the detail. It was Thom Hartmann who eventually unearthed the original records in Vermont only to find that the judge had specifically stated that the case did not relate to corporate personhood. The headnote had been written a year after the hearing by the Recorder, a person whose life had been with the railroads. By then the judge was too ill to check the headnote. **American corporate law is therefore based on a fraud.**

I thought Americans admired their founders

The second step to corporate tyranny was adoption by the US of the WTO and NAFTA agreements. It is commonly thought that these benefit the United States. Wrong. The agreements deprive US citizens and authorities of the ability to make decisions about their local environment and trade, giving power to foreign bureaucrats who meet in secret. NAFTA's effect on Mexico, where eight million fell from the middle class into poverty, has been well documented. But in the US 2.6 million jobs vanished (many to be replaced by part-time or low-pay service sector jobs), workers lost $28 billion in bonuses, wages fell 28%, working hours increased, environmental laws were overruled and the trade deficit soared. It was only corporations that benefited, through being able to overturn local laws and force down the cost of labour.

All the protections against corporate power sought by the American Founders have been lost. Corporations, with the right to 'personhood', now have the right to meet and influence 'their' elected representatives. Chemical corporations, quoting the Santa Clara case, claim the right to privacy to prevent uninvited inspections of their toxic sites by the Environmental Protection Agency. Corporations have the right to sue an objector at a public meeting for, say, slander and frequently exercise it, not hoping to win but to intimidate with the threat of legal fees. Corporations, asserting the right to free speech, used a perverse advertising campaign to kill off Clinton's proposal for health-care protection to the 40 million uninsured.

Can the US return to the values of its Founders? Reversal of the Santa Clara case would be the first step to subjecting corporations to the control of the people. The federal government, each state, each township, could then regulate corporations to the benefit of its citizens and help local economies to flourish once again. Indeed, in California local governments have already passed laws that deny corporations the status of persons, while in Pennsylvania some townships have forbidden corporations from owning or controlling farms in their communities.

Huge questions remain. Deprived of personhood the corporations would still have financial bully-power. But, because of its unique constitution, the United States could lead the world once again towards government of the people by the people, for the people (not by and for corporations).

Contributions for 1996 elections:

96% of Americans	$0
the next 3.75%	up to $200
top 500 corporations	over $500,000 each

In 1998 elections the top 500 corporations gave $660,000,000 to candidates.

Unequal Protection
Thom Hartmann 2002

Civilised Values

for culture, environment and peace?

"Why do they hate us?" asked George W Bush following 9/11. Only by understanding its cause can we hope to avoid provoking more hatred.

Americans have civilised values, are deeply democratic by instinct, disrespectful of authority by nature, very conscious of their freedoms, and happy to live in a vast and beautiful land free from external threats. However, their representatives have jettisoned much of this precious baggage.

Hatred feeds on stories. In November 1990, a fifteen-year-old Kuwaiti girl testified to Congress in tears that she had seen soldiers ripping out wires and tossing premature babies onto the floor so that incubators could be sent back to Iraq. Her heart-rending testimony was a crucial factor in persuading Congress to approve the first war with Iraq. It later transpired that this was a fabrication and the girl had been trained in her performance by the PR firm Hill & Knowlton. **Official statements are now simply PR exercises.**

Some stories are suppressed. "Al-Jazeera has an editorial line and a way of presenting news that appeals to the Arab public," said Colin Powell, "It tends to portray our efforts in a negative light." The US bombed this independent Arab station's headquarters in both Afghanistan and Baghdad, killing reporters, and it wiped Al-Jazeera's sites off the Internet.

In 1945 the US exterminated 200,000 children, women and men in Hiroshima and Nagasaki. In the US story this ended WW2. In other stories the US wished to frighten Russia and compare two different WMDs before the chance was lost. Now that the US again feels safe from retaliation the Nuclear Posture Review identifies Russia, China, North Korea, Iraq, Iran, Syria and Libya as potential targets for pre-emptive nuclear strikes.

During the Cold War the US subverted any government promoting land reform or other social programmes. It armed and supported dictators like Marcos in the Philippines, the Shah in Iran, Batista in Cuba, Pinochet in Chile, Mobuto in Zaire, Suharto in Indonesia, Savimbi in Angola – the list is endless and the numbers that died as a consequence of US interventions are measured in millions. In the US story it was holding an evil empire at bay. **In the majority nations' story it destroyed all hope of social programmes in many Asian, African and American countries.** The only state that had a reformist, often communist, government and escaped US attentions was Kerala in India and it shows what might have been achieved elsewhere.

In Vietnam, both sides used intimidation, terror, torture and assassinations. Neighbouring Laos was subjected to the heaviest bombing campaign in history – half a ton of ordnance for every man, woman and child – plus defoliants and herbicides on forests, rice paddies, farmers' fields, lakes, rivers and ponds making the water unsuitable for cultivation or drinking. Unexploded ordnance still mutilates 200 people each year. At the time, American citizens were told that Agent Orange "only hurts the plants;" but it was the largest chemical warfare campaign in history. 650,000 children in Vietnam, even today, suffer horrific deformities and torturing pain as a result.

In Nicaragua the US armed and supported the Contras, a terrorist group. For eight terrible years the people suffered all-out war aimed at destroying the progressive social and economic programmes of the government. The Contras burned down schools and medical clinics, raping, torturing, bombing, mining harbours and fixing elections. The economy was destroyed. The CIA used corrupt or criminal banks for this operation. But when Contra activities had become too notorious Congress banned further funding and the gap was filled with drugs money under CIA protection. The US has carried out terrorist actions against Cuba for over 40 years. The Kennedy/Schlesinger papers reveal that the US feared the social programmes of countries like Cuba might prove popular and lead to "successful defiance of US policies." Aggression from these countries was never even an issue.

In 1998 the US destroyed Sudan's only pharmaceutical factory thus denying basic drugs to millions. Hundreds of thousands have died prematurely and hatred of the US has escalated. In Malawi a million people may die because the US blocked the release of affordable drugs from India. The astronomic price of narcotics on the streets of Western cities distorts the agriculture and governance of countries like Afghanistan and Colombia. The US blames drugs barons, supports oppressive governments and sprays foreign fields with bio-agents. But global inequality is the real cause.

The US is the only country in the world to be indicted by the World Court for crimes against humanity. It gives sanctuary to notorious criminals: Morales responsible for torture and massacre, José Garcia who ran death squads, General Prosper Avril who liked to display his victims of torture on television, Armando Larios responsible for tortures and executions in Chile, Pol Pot's henchman Thiounn Prasith, Cuban plane hijackers – and many more.

The US School of the Americas was the world's leading university of terrorism. Its training manuals recommend and give detailed instructions for blackmail, kidnap, ridicule, humiliation, deception, false statements, torture, murder, arrests of witnesses' relatives, how to give rise to reprisals and rape, how to turn peaceful demonstrations violent, planting evidence, targeting key people, use of criminals, 'friendly' assassination to create martyrs etc. Stories of torture and endless solitary confinement at Guantanamo – with the military as judge, jury and prosecutor – are not difficult to believe.

When Madeleine Albright was asked whether the death of 500,000 Iraqi children due to sanctions against Iraq was a price worth paying, she replied: "I think this is a very hard choice, but the price – we think the price is worth it."

"I'm amazed that there is so much misunderstanding of what our country is about that people would hate us. I just can't believe it, because I know how good we are."
George W Bush

"I'd like to be able to go somewhere in the world and not have to apologise for being from the United States."
Pres. Bishop of the Episcopalian Church

The Empire

full spectrum absurdity

"All this talk about first we do Afghanistan, then we do Iraq... this is entirely the wrong way to go about it. If we just let our vision of the world go forth, and we embrace it entirely and we don't try to piece together clever diplomacy, but just wage total war... our children will sing great songs about us years from now."
Richard Perle 2003.

The US is the world's only hyperpower. It, with the élite of other countries, is undertaking a vast project to reorganise the world through an economy based on corporate market fundamentalism with common cultural values and western style democracy. All nations must conform, whether they like it or not,

The 'War on Terror' has replaced the Cold War so that US exploitation of world resources, backed by military force, can continue. In the ten years following the Cold War the US embarked on 48 military interventions to promote American interests in other people's countries. Following 9/11, the President secured unlimited war powers free from Congressional accountability to target countries at will on the merest suspicion of harbouring terrorists. This is accompanied at home by curbs on civil liberties, the crushing of domestic dissent, a new era of indefinite secrecy for presidential records and the criminalisation of legitimate protest.

The Project for the New American Century (PNAC) set out the blueprint for the development of this empire in June 1997. Later, in September 2000, the PNAC said, "The process of transformation, even if it brings revolutionary change, is likely to be a long one, absent some catastrophic and catalysing event – like a new Pearl Harbour." One year later 9/11 was the defining event (just as the Indian Mutiny led to the British Empire or the burning of the Reichstag confirmed Hitler in power). The decisions to invade Afghanistan and Iraq were made before, not after, 11th September.

The dominant position of the US could have provided peace and stability through cooperation with other nations in a world of weak governments, corrupt global corporations and anti-élite radical groups. Its economy has stimulated trade when most others were stagnant or collapsing. Its communications science has made the world into a global village, though of questionable cultural value.

But the US has chosen to act outside international law. Examples are legion and include refusing to sign the Kyoto Protocol, violating the Montreal Protocol on ozone, rejecting the Clean Energy Plan, rejecting the Comprehensive Test Ban Treaty, withdrawal from the ABM Treaty, violating and killing the Biological and Toxic Weapons Convention, refusing inspection of its weapons of mass destruction, refusing to sign a treaty on the rights of the child, 'un-signing' the treaty for an International Criminal Court, ignoring the Geneva Convention. The list of rejections goes on: Land Mines – Small Arms – Weaponisation of Space – Business Corruption – Law of the Sea – Economic Espionage – Harmful Tax Competition – Racism. Above all, the US doctrine, supported by Britain, allowing pre-emptive strikes introduces a new era of international lawlessness.

After Hitler's war the United Nations established unanimously "that to initiate a war of aggression [unsanctioned by international treaty] is not only an international crime, it is the supreme international crime differing only from other war crimes in that it contains within itself the accumulated evil of the whole." Nazi leaders were held personally responsible and hanged for this crime. No international treaty sanctioned the pre-emptive and unprovoked invasion and occupation of Iraq or the handing of its assets to US companies.

The life-blood of the Empire is oil, so the US must have control over oil production if it is to maintain its global hegemony. The world's biggest oil reserves are in the Middle East where the US now has 27 military bases. The Caspian/Gulf zone, sometimes referred to as the 51st state, is at the heart of the land mass that includes China, the

Indian sub-continent, Indonesia, the Middle East, Africa, Europe and Russia. Oil and gas pipelines radiate from here. With control of this zone the US can threaten the economy of these countries. China is the endgame being the workshop of the world but with an uncertain commitment to the empire project. China is dependent on imports for two-thirds of its energy so has a legitimate fear of US rhetoric.

The US now seeks universal hegemony through military power. **The mission statement of its armed forces is 'full spectrum dominance',** dominance on land, of the oceans, of the airwaves and intelligence, and in space. Since the Cold War, the US has revised its policy to achieve control of the planet, it has reduced its army but increased expenditure on intercontinental-range bombers, the Navy's long-range strike capabilities, forward deployment of supplies especially in the Gulf and the Indian Ocean and setting up counter-insurgency groups in 50 countries.

The US aims to revolutionise warfare with directed-energy, space-based laser weapons, invulnerable satellites circling the earth, able to target any stationary or moving object on the ground, in the air or in space at the speed of light and with extreme precision. "The globalisation of the world economy," says the US Space Command's 'Vision for 2020' report, "will continue with a widening between haves and have-nots. From space the US would keep those have-nots in line." And the Commander-in-Chief of Space Command said, "We're going to fight *in* space. We're going to fight *from* space and we're going to fight *into* space" (his emphasis).

Friendly states provide moral support and help with bases and intelligence facilities but their interests will be ignored when they are no longer considered friendly or useful. France found this when it questioned the legality of the invasion of Iraq, and Britain will be similarly sidelined when it has a leader not totally committed to the US empire. Less friendly states suffer economic or military aggression. Poor countries, like the 35 that refused to guarantee the immunity of US citizens from prosecution, have had aid terminated.

However, the reliance on overwhelming power and technical wizardry meets untidy human complications. Arming the Northern Alliance against the Taliban in Afghanistan spread arms to warlords who fight the US-imposed government. The opium trade, banned by the Taliban, is now healthier than ever. The invasion of Iraq has opened the country to al-Qa'eda and recruited thousands to its cause, an objective perhaps behind the 11th September atrocity. The empire's ability to conquer has been demonstrated but its attempts at keeping peace have been counter-productive. Fundamentalist groups within the US, that equate current events with Biblical prophesies of Armageddon, twist logic so that peacemaking is seen as contrary to God's will.

The US position is simple: the interests of the United States are not negotiable and, in the words of George W. Bush, **"You are either with us or against us."**

> *"Facism should more properly be called corporatism, since it is the merger of state and corporate power."*
> Benito Mussolini, fascist dictator
> 1925-43

The infrastructure of the US is crumbling - electric grid, roads, schools, water treatment, hazardous waste – these are denied funding while funds are poured into Iraq. This may be because, at home, all contracts are tendered and scrutinised while in Iraq they can be handed to cronies that contribute to party funds. The stink of corruption floats over the stench of mutilation and genetic defects resulting from military aggression that used cluster bombs and radioactive ordnance.

If the purpose was to remove an evil dictator, why is Karimov of Uzbekistan such a friend and why did Britain withdraw its ambassador for criticising his evil ways? Answer: the US was allowed a military presence in Uzbekistan but denied it in Iraq.

Military expenditure

Imperial Tribute

why the rich are rich and the majority poor

The United States creates dollars, bits of paper or computer entries that don't cost anything to make, for other people to use. These are its biggest export. Professor Thomas Barnett of the US Naval War College explained the process: "We trade little pieces of paper (our currency, in the form of a trade deficit) for Asia's amazing array of products and services. We are smart enough to know this is patently an unfair deal unless we offer something of great value along with those little pieces of paper. The product is a strong US Pacific fleet, which squares the transaction nicely." In other words, in exchange for vast quantities of goods and services, the poor get a US military presence. Big deal!

What is real wealth? People grow food and flowers, mine minerals, refine them, design and make things, create art and music, run businesses and do all those things that make a country tick. These are the things that make for a good life and trade. But the US does not export as many of these things as it imports. A third of its exports are simply – dollars. **The ability of the US to export an international currency in exchange for real wealth is one reason why most of the world is poor and the United States is rich.**

People want these dollars because they have become an international currency. A sheikh gets dollars for the oil he sells the US. He might buy a skyscraper in Sydney as an investment. The Australian, in turn, may buy goods from Japan using the dollars. The Japanese may set up a factory in the US. So the dollars circulate. The more trade there is, the better for the US because people will want more dollars. Countries, also, need a cushion. So there are dollars in central banks, in businesses and in private accounts all round the world. Many of them invested back in US treasury bonds where they finance US wars.

The amount of these exported dollars, the net foreign liability, is huge, $2,500 billion. This is in effect an interest-free loan, maybe a gift, from the poor to the most opulent country on earth (it would cost only $40 billion a year for 10 years to ensure that everyone in the world had adequate diet, safe water, basic healthcare, adequate sanitation and natal care).

In order to support its standard of living the US must export $2bn of currency every day (the trade deficit). The US wants trade throughout the world to increase so that people will need these dollars. It is annoyed with Japan for failing to get its economy going. It is annoyed with Europe for not growing fast enough. It wants poor nations to cultivate cash crops for export rather than for local use. And it insists that heavily indebted poor countries will only have their debts cancelled if they open their markets to global free trade.

Is the bubble already bursting?

If the desire for dollars reduces, their value will drop. **The US will no longer enjoy a free lunch.** But its exports will become competitive, its internal economy will flourish making the things it no longer receives as a gift from the poor, and its debt will reduce in value (a benefit denied to poor indebted countries). Ironically, this loss of income could ensure a healthy future.

Some countries are already trading oil in euros thus reducing the need for dollars. Saudi Arabia would withdraw its US investments if threatened so the country that supplied terrorists for 11th September was spared. In 2003, under the Patriot Act, the US transferred $1.7 billion of Iraqi assets to the US Federal Reserve Bank; will the US also steal China's deposits? After all, George W Bush refers to China as part of the 'axis of evil.'

The perverse international financial architecture started at Bretton Woods in 1944 when the US was given the right to have its dollars considered the equivalent of gold in the reserves of central banks throughout the world. General de Gaulle of France called it "an exorbitant privilege" though the value of the privilege was limited while the dollar was linked to gold. But in 1971 President Nixon broke this link and the privilege is now unconstrained. Europe would like its own strong currency so that it can pick up the loot as the dollar drops. It is difficult to understand how such an iniquitous arrangement has been allowed to run for half a century and is still in place.

John Maynard Keynes said at Bretton Woods that **there should be a currency for trade between nations that is independent of any national currency.** He was overruled. Sixty years on, his recommendation should be revisited. An independent international currency need not be dependent on the consent of the US. The process could start with a few countries, say the G21, exchanging products using an invented international currency. As dollar reserves are released the advantages would become obvious and others would join in. But with the prospect that another currency, euro or yen, might overtake the dollar the US may realise that an international currency could be in its interest.

And Then?

Many see the future with the Japan/China axis if it can learn to live within a finite planet. Western politicians regard these two nations as enemies of each other. Flat-earth economists look only at the financial sector and consider Japan a basket case. They fail to see its successes, its investment in key modern industry and infrastructure, its trading surpluses, its high savings rate and rising living standards. Japan assumes China will be the world's biggest economy and is lowering import and export trade barriers both ways while keeping them high to others. India could be an equal player, with expertise in a growing service sector, and Malaysia could contribute its economic sophistication.

Thirty years ago the US had a plan for 'funding the dollar overhang' into the world monetary system. Other countries would get IMF credit equal to their dollar holdings, but these would no longer be US Treasury obligations. In other words, the US debt would be cancelled. And when OPEC countries proposed moving dollars out of Federal bonds to corporate bonds they were told this would be considered and act of war. But the debt is now so huge, these measures can no longer be considered.

Biomimicry

science's exciting new frontier

A certain spider *(nephila clavipes)* makes six different kinds of silk. When hit by a fast-flying moth the silk can stretch by 40% and then return to its original size unaffected. The US army is researching spiders because their web is stronger and has better energy-absorbing elasticity than Kevlar, a fibre so tough that it can stop bullets. Kevlar is made by pouring petroleum-derived molecules into a pressurised vat of concentrated sulphuric acid to be boiled at several hundred degrees and then subjected to high pressures. A spider just needs a fly or two.

A hummingbird can fly forwards, backwards, up, down or sideways, with equal ease. It can fly across the Gulf of Mexico on three grams of fuel and, when picking up its fuel, fertilise the flower to provide more fuel in future. Compare the resources consumed and the damage done in building and flying a Chinook. We have a lot to learn. Architects are fascinated by the ability of termites to build structures that maintain a constant temperature in their interior chambers. Computer scientists think that ants might help them with parallel, rather than linear, computers. And if we want a lot of hydrogen, now that we are entering the hydrogen economy, nature makes it all the time with the help of an enzyme. Can we mimic nature?

Material scientists boast about the incredibly high pressure they can achieve to make hard ceramics (an oyster beats them), high temperatures for special steels, and elaborate chemical processes (they can't match a mollusk for underwater glue). Theirs is outmoded Stone Age technology – *heat, beat and treat*. Some agricultural researchers are noticing that nature does not use the plough. Plants naturally grow as mixed communities, with seldom fewer than four species together. Nature favours perennials. Even organic farming still has a lot to learn from nature.

Then energy. Almost all our energy comes from the sun – via plants. Coal and oil are embodied energy captured millions of years ago. **Duckweed captures solar energy with 95% efficiency, many times better than man-made photovoltaic cells.** A leaf takes in water and carbon dioxide, the carbon forms sugars that store the sun's energy and oxygen is given off. But how? Scientists say 'membrane potential' where a positive electron is moved to one side of a membrane and a negative electron to the other. If we could mimic that, and if the process needed no more inputs than stagnant water and daylight and produced no more waste than duckweed produces, we would have a truly sustainable energy source. The scientific race is on.

Genetic knowledge is the biggest recent leap forward but experience suggests that immensely powerful new technologies should be approached with caution. Fossil fuels, while making possible the lifestyle we value, have been largely responsible for overpopulation, degraded land, changing climate, rising sea levels and resource wars. We are on a unique planet on which life has evolved in a unique way and we must live within the planet's unique patterns. In three billion years, all sorts of diverse properties have been combined, like crystals and membranes in a spider's web. But not everything. Boundaries have been erected, and it is these boundaries that we are excitedly destroying when taking genetic inheritance into our own hands. The most pressing need is to recognise how use can be made of genetic knowledge without upsetting three billion years of evolution. Novel genes may cause havoc as they move vertically and horizontally through future generations of bacteria, plants, animals, and ourselves.

Biomimicry introduces an era based, not on what we can extract from nature, but on what we can learn from her. 'Doing it nature's way' has the potential to change the way we educate our children, grow food, make materials, harness energy, heal ourselves, store information and conduct business.

Biomimicry
Janine M Benyus 1997

Soil

storehouse of nutrition

In a spoonful of healthy soil there can be a billion organisms from over 10,000 species. Soil is alive – a mineral, animal and vegetable kingdom under the more visible green canopy of nature. It is the storehouse from which plants extract resources and in which they lay down reserves for the future. Scientific understanding of the way plants use the soil seems to be in its infancy, comparable with physics about a hundred years ago when the realisation dawned that there was power in the atomic structure of matter.

A single worm can shift 30 tons of earth in its lifetime. Together with insects the worms aerate the ground, drag rotting material down, digest and excrete it, and begin the process of transforming it into humus. Bacteria, fungi, protozoa and algae then get to work and release the nutrients from the humus as minerals, proteins, carbohydrates and sugars. Plants extract up to 10,000 naturally occurring compounds, known as phytonutrients, which nourish them and protect them from pests and disease.

Then there are mycorrhizae, the white fuzz around the plant roots. Mycorrhizae create a living bridge between the plant, the minerals and the microbial community with organic acids in a two-way process. The plants grow and feed insects and other animals. Then falling plant matter and manure is deposited onto the soil, returning the nutrients that the plants extracted. The cycle of life continues and the topsoil becomes richer. Beware of simplistic statements about our food. Sir Albert Howard, one of the first agricultural scientists to appreciate these systems, came to the conclusion that "the maintenance of the fertility of the soil is the first condition of any system of permanent agriculture."

Through most of history, farmers have worked with nature, noticing when things go wrong. Sometimes things went badly wrong. In the Fertile Crescent of the Middle East, rising salts destroyed both the crops and the empires that depended on them. In the Roman Empire, returning generals invested wealth from conquests in farms and ran them with managers and slaves. Farmers became soldiers and their indigenous knowledge went with them. Rome declined and fell and the fertility of peninsular Italy has never recovered. Things went badly wrong last century with industrial farming when wealth again concentrated land and control into a few hands. Traditional and local knowledge was lost; machines assumed the role that slaves had in Rome and the world lost much of its topsoil.

The quality of what remains is deteriorating. Since 1940, the iron in spinach has dropped 60%, broccoli has lost 75% of its calcium, carrots have lost 75% of their magnesium, watercress has lost 93% of its copper – the list goes on. Selenium, potassium, phosphorus, iodine, molybdenum, sodium, chromium, manganese – over 20 trace minerals have been analysed and the quantity of all of them has been diminishing in a wide variety

of fruit and vegetables. It is these minerals that help keep plants healthy, that are essential constituents of our bones, teeth, muscle, soft tissue, blood and nerve cells; minerals that are involved in almost all the body's metabolic processes. The loss of these elements in our food may have contributed to the massive increase in allergies in the UK.

With increasing knowledge one would expect agricultural science to have found ways to correct this trend. But the reverse is happening.

The Little Food Book
Craig Sams 2003

Feeding the World

there is no shortage of money or food

The Royal Society and the National Academy of Sciences, the leading scientific bodies of Britain and the US, said in a joint report in July 2000:

"Modern agriculture is intrinsically destructive of the environment. It is particularly destructive of biological diversity. The widespread application of conventional agricultural technologies such as herbicides, pesticides, fertilisers and tillage has resulted in severe environmental damage in many parts of the world."

At the beginning of the last century, most food was grown and distributed locally. At its end, just 20 multinational corporations dominated a food trade that had gone international. In spite of this, well over half the population in poor countries is still in farming families. So the most effective way to feed the majority of the world's poor is to ensure that small farmers have good access to local markets, that they have secure land rights and are not forced to sell, do not have to buy seed, are helped with appropriate research and technology and have control over water in their locality. Their sales must not be undercut by subsidised imports or by supermarkets exploiting the defenceless.

Two-fifths of the world population is malnourished. Half of these are hungry. The other half eats too much unhealthy junk food. This is hardly surprising because most nutrition research is now funded by and for agribusiness. It is in their interest to develop and advertise food that will appeal to the rich not the poor, to encourage growing for export rather than to meet local needs, to make farmers dependent on purchased seed, chemicals, and machinery. It is not in their interest to help farmers to be self-sufficient.

There is no world shortage of food. The US has huge surpluses. India exports grain and meat to wealthy countries and even considers dumping excess grain at sea. Poverty, not lack of food, in an increasingly wealthy and unequal world, condemns **a billion people to live daily with the horror that they and their families may not have enough, or anything, to eat.**

The twenty companies that dominate the food trade would like us to believe that increasingly specialised crops, genetic engineering and new chemicals are required to feed the world, not just to fill their pockets.

Risk from chemical farming.
Arable land is constantly being lost because chemicals destroy the quality of soil. Dependence on chemicals puts poor farmers in debt and drives them off the land. Nitrates seep into ground and poison drinking water. Persistent synthetic chemicals (POPs and EDCs) endanger human and animal health and reproduction. Chemical run-off pollutes coastal waters. The short-term advantage of herbicides and pesticides soon turns into a long-term hazard as resistance develops and the balance of predators is upset.

Risk from monoculture.
Diversity is fundamental to all life. The current use of only high-yield crops is a tendency towards monoculture, so is contrary to sound science. During the 20th century three-quarters of the genetic diversity of agricultural crops was lost, 100,000 varieties of rice have been reduced to a few dozen, and three-quarters of the world's rice now descends from a single plant. The Irish experience with potatoes was just one warning that monoculture is the herald of starvation.

Risk from specialisation.
Crops are increasingly produced where they can be grown cheaply and transported around the world. This creates single-crop farming which makes the whole crop vulnerable. When farmers grow a cash crop for export rather than local sustenance the local economy is made hostage to the global economy.

Risk from dependence.
Industrial agriculture is dependent on phosphorus for fertiliser and on oil for chemicals, distribution and machinery. Both are limited resources. Both will escalate in price. And, being a major user of fossil fuels, industrial farming helps to destroy the

climate on which all cultivation depends. The predicted 3ft rise in sea levels will swamp 30% of the world's cropland.

Risk from reliance on imports.

When societies take unnecessary supplies from abroad, the security of their food is put at risk. Cheap wheat, subsidised by the US, is bankrupting thousands of poor farmers. Britain imports apples and as a result has lost most of its orchards. European dairy products are destroying local production in milk-rich Mongolia. Dutch butter costs less than Kenyan butter in the shops of Nairobi. Imports of food should be restricted to what cannot be grown, or cannot be grown in sufficient quantities, locally.

Risk from 'productivity'.

There are two ways of measuring productivity. First: what one person can produce. Secondly what one acre can produce. Big business uses the first measure and in poor countries this drives small farmers off the land to city slums (by 2030 it is predicted that a third of the world will be slumdwellers). What matters is the second measure, productivity per acre. The most productive land is the vegetable plot of an enthusiast who feeds her family and gives or sells to neighbours. Large-scale production for supermarkets is the least productive since intercropping is not possible and anything not absolutely uniform must be discarded. Between these two, productivity per acre reduces as size increases. The highly productive intensive rearing of animals, like battery chickens, apart from being horrifically cruel, is dependent on the use of antibiotic prophylactics and has the inherent risk of viruses spreading out of control.

In Britain, government and the Food Standards Agency's obsession with chemical-based agribusiness and low shelf price, together with their neglect of small and organic farms, is discouraging principled growers and endangering the sustainability and health of our food supply.

An family of four pays £11 a week to remedy agrichemical pollution and £16 for subsidies to intensive farmers. Food poisoning rose from 14,000 cases in 1982 to 106,000 cases in 1998. This is only a part of the price we pay for cheap food in supermarkets.

The absurd food swap

pork:	exports	195,000 tonnes
	imports	240,000 tonnes

lamb:	exports	102,000 tonnes
	imports	125,000 tonnes

butter:	exports	49,000 tonnes
	imports	47,000 tonnes

fresh milk:	exports	119,000 tonnes
	imports:	114,000 tonnes

poultry meat:	exports	170,000 tonnes
	imports	363,000 tonnes

(40,000 tonnes in 2003 came from Thailand where the avian flu virus is rampant)

UK live pigs:	exports	110,000 pigs
	imports	200,000 pigs

(long-distance transport of live animals should be banned on grounds of cruelty)

The absurd food swap apparently makes sense to flat-earth economists, but it spreads disease and contributes to global warming.

42% of rural parishes in Britain have no shop, 43% have no post office, 49% have no school, 75% have no daily bus service and 83% have no doctor. This is a direct result of low-labour industrial farming.

52,000 farmers went out of business in Britain in 2002. Our government said that farmers need to form soviet-style collectives in order to compete in world markets.

CO_2 emissions from transporting 1kg of apples:
- from New Zealand: 1,000 grams
- locally grown: 50 grams

Airfreight should be phased out altogether

Most Germans would rather die than become vegetarian. But industrial farming may force them. Their beef and venison may harbour BSE, their sheep scrapie, their chickens may be laced with salmonella and their pork may contain antibiotic steroids that could give women hairy chests. At Kreuzberg Zoo the staff were so desperate for healthy meat they resorted to eating the zoo's prize poultry.

🌱 With intensified use of pesticides in the US the proportion of crops lost to pests has increased from 32% to 37%. Many pests are now resistant to pesticides.

🌱 For mixed farming straw and dung combine as fertiliser. For large-scale intensive farming they are both problems for disposal.

🌱 The tendency to eat more meat is not sustainable. Ten acres can produce either one ton of beef or between 50 nd 100 tons of grains, pulses and vegetables.

The Great Fruit Salad Story

Fruit salad from tree to table by modern, industrial, unsafe, irrational, quasi-scientific, bureaucratically controlled, fuel-inefficient, economically perverse, farming and distribution methods. An indigenous person expends one calorie to get four calories of food. How much energy is used to get four calories of food now?

The Great Food Gamble
John Humphreys 2001

Organics

respecting nature's way

In 1896 Professor Shaler of Harvard University said: "If mankind can't devise and enforce ways of dealing with the earth which will preserve the source of life, we must look forward to a time when our kind, having wasted its inheritance, will fade from the earth." **America has now lost half its topsoil.** It can take at least 500 years to develop an inch of topsoil, so the damage is immense.

Eve Balfour, one of the founders of the Soil Association, a woman in the man's world of mid-century agriculture, saw land as a fountain of energy flowing through a circuit of soils, plants and animals. She defined food as living channels that conduct energy upwards, while death and decay return it to the soil. In 1946 she warned that chemicals like DDT would get into, and work their way up, the food chain. This hazard took 50 years to enter the consciousness of administrators.

Twenty years later a scientist, Rachel Carson, wrote *Silent Spring* and thus helped to start the ecology movement. It warned of a countryside depopulated, devoid of wildlife and devastated by chemicals. Since then, man's attack on nature has intensified to all-out warfare as tractors compact the soil, herbicides destroy the humus, and pesticides kill micro-organisms, insects and natural predators. If agricultural scientists claim credit for improving the yield of specialised crops then they must also admit responsibility for the tragic results of their myopic interventions. At last, at the opening of a new century, the general public is beginning to realise that our inheritance hangs in the balance.

When a farmer changes from chemical to organic farming, the productivity of his farm immediately drops. This is because chemicals have degraded the soil and killed predators. It takes several years to restore the land to full productivity. Comparative studies for corn, wheat, soybeans and tomatoes have found that fully restored organic fields average between 94 and 100% of the yields of nearby conventional crops. But these comparisons ignore size. The smaller the farm the greater the yield. A small organic farm with mixed crops, intercropping and animals can have a considerably higher yield than large conventional farms. This is the farming that can do most to feed the world and can prevent farmers from being uprooted.

Eve Balfour linked the land with our mental, social and spiritual experience. She insisted that contact between town and country should be encouraged, and that farming should be an integral aspect of education. It will be many years before this vision of truly organic sustenance can become a reality. It bears very little resemblance to 'supermarket organic' which uses planes and lorries to move produce around world.

Over the past decade sales of organic produce has been the fastest growing sector in British and US agriculture. It is already 95% as productive as conventional farming in spite of the subsidies and research the latter receives. If a fraction of that support were given to organic growing it would be more productive.

Why is organic produce more expensive? Because the market is distorted. Market fundamentalism does not apply when agribusiness can influence the government. Society, not the farmers, carries the costs of pesticide contamination, polluted water and other health, chemical-management and environmental impacts associated with industrial farming – not to mention the massive subsidies to big-scale farmers. Organic food represents the true cost of food in an undistorted economy.

Cuba, through necessity, provides some interesting lessons. The trade embargo and the collapse of the former Soviet Union meant that it could not import fertilisers, pesticides or fuel for tractors. Most of the food in Cuba is grown in *huertos*, private urban plots of less than a quarter of an acre, and sold from stalls on pavements, at street corners and under the covered walkways of Havana's elegant, crumbling colonial buildings. Inside the city, chemical fertilisers and pesticides are forbidden and compost is made from household waste.

The government took up the challenge of a local, science-based, low input, sustainable agriculture. Unused city land was given to anyone who wanted to cultivate. Forty percent of state farms became co-operatives while the rest were divided into small units. Thousands of jobs were created, 200,000 in 2001 alone. "The secret is in the high productivity," said Nelso Compagnioni of the Institute for Tropical Agriculture. "Every dollar of produce on a small plot costs 25 cents to produce; as soon as you increase the area you get higher costs. And we have no need for transport; customers collect their food on the way home from work."

What will happen when sanctions are lifted? Will neo-liberalism destroy it all? "There will be tough negotiations" says Mavis Alvares, director of the Association of Small Farmers, "it simply isn't the policy of the government to have cheap imported food. We've put an immense educational effort into sustainability."

Sloppy farming practice in Britain resulted in mad cow disease and the horrors of CJD, the human equivalent. Organic farmers had not been allowed to feed animal protein to ruminants since 1983, three years before the first case, and there have been no recorded cases of BSE in any animal born and reared organically. Organic farming bans irradiation and estrogen-mimicking pesticides (POPs and EDCs). In contrast, non-organic food can have more than 500 food additives.

For three months in 2003 in Britain 10% of all eggs were contaminated with dangerous drugs, like lasalocid sodium, which are used to control parasites on birds that are kept in overcrowded conditions. The public was not told.

The Soil Association
www.soilassociation.org

A Citizens' Jury

the locals know what aid they need

Anjamma is a farmer who works four acres of land with her children. They have two bullocks, eight buffalo and no machines. She was one of 12 people chosen to take part in a citizens' jury of small traders, small and marginal farmers, food processors and consumers to assess ambitious plans for farming in their part of India.

The Chief Minister of Andhra Pradesh, Chandrababu Naidu, has been widely acclaimed for the state's modernising achievements with Information Technology. If IT, why not agriculture? US agricultural advisers were brought in and Vision 2020 was drawn up, to bring millions of poor farmers straight into the 21st century with massive consolidation of farms, mechanisation of agriculture, irrigation projects, new roads and the introduction of genetically modified crops. The state government claims that the programme will eradicate poverty.

The Citizens' Jury sat through days of evidence from politicians, seed companies, academics, aid donors and NGOs in June 2001. Three scenarios were presented and advocates for each tried to persuade the jury that their particular approach would provide the best opportunity to enhance livelihoods and food security in the coming twenty years. An oversight panel checked that each proposal was presented in a fair and unprejudiced way.

The first proposal was the State's Vision 2020. The second was for environmentally-friendly farming to meet western demands for organic and fair-trade produce. The third was based on increased self-reliance for rural communities, low input, local food production and local marketing. The jury could either choose one of the pre-formed visions or promote its own unique view. Its verdict was very clear:

- They wanted encouragement for self-reliance and community control over resources.
- They gave priority to the maintenance of healthy soils (the farmers among them were conscious of the harmful legacy of pesticides and fertilisers).
- They wanted to maintain diverse crops, trees and livestock.
- They wanted to build on indigenous knowledge, skills and local institutions
- They wanted to maintain control of medicinal plants and their export.

And their opposition was clearly expressed:

- They were horrified that Vision 2020's proposals would reduce those working the land from 70 to 40% in Andhra Pradesh. This would uproot 20 million people, leaving them with no livelihood.
- They did not want genetically modified crops, specifically not 'Vitamin A' rice, nor 'Bt cotton'.
- They did not want consolidation of ownership into fewer and bigger farms for cash crops.
- They did not want an increase in contract farming.

- They did not want labour-displacing machinery.

Anjamma was asked what she would do if Vision 2020 goes ahead. "There will be nothing for us to do", she replied, "other than to drink pesticides and die."

In the US the Jefferson Centre has conducted citizens' juries since 1974 covering a wide variety of issues like property tax reform, assisted suicide, environmental risks, traffic congestion pricing, agriculture and water policy, electricity futures and many more.

Citizens seem more intelligent than governments

We all believe in democracy but we all know that decision-makers are swayed by lobbyists or activists. The Citizens Jury provides an unparalleled opportunity for a group of citizens to learn about an issue from experts, and for legislators to hear the people's authentic voice. It has worked well in such diverse countries as the US, Germany and India, and sceptics have been surprised at the positive and sensible outcome of these juries.

www.ids.ac.uk

POPs & EDCs

synthetic time bombs

In January 1999, in Belgium, two gallons of transformer oil were accidentally mixed with fats destined for cattle feed. The oil contained two synthetic compounds, PCBs and furans. Ten feed manufacturers sold their products to 1,700 farmers, who gave them to countless chickens, pigs, and cows.

Although the exposure in each mouthful of feed was minuscule, the contaminants concentrate in animal fat. By the end of May, retailers throughout Belgium dumped all poultry and egg products, farms slaughtered any animals suspected of carrying the poisons and governments throughout the world banned importation of all Belgian animal products.

PCBs and furans are POPs, persistent organic pollutants, and POPs are a legacy of the agrichemical revolution. They revolutionised farming. They kill pests and increase food production. The benefits were so widespread that anyone questioning their use was accused of being anti-science, obstructing agricultural and industrial progress and depriving the poor of protection against disease (exactly what politicians are saying in defence of genetic engineering today). The Royal Society now says that POPs and other synthetic chemicals have caused severe damage around the world.

We should not be surprised. These chemicals were developed for explosives and nerve gases during World War II. At the end of the war the chemical companies were left with huge over capacity so they lobbied. And they succeeded. **They diverted their weapons against people to weapons against the land.** Not surprisingly, fifty years of chemical attack have degraded the soil and damaged the nation's health.

Synthetic chemicals are new to nature. They have not formed part of life's evolutionary process so they offend the first principle of sustainability. They are now found everywhere, even in the Antarctic. And they are working their way up the food chain from gulls and fish to seals and eagles. They accumulate so that we all now have 500 synthetic chemicals in our bodies. Mothers have many, including dioxin and PCBs, in their breast milk. POPs cause cancer.

It is not possible to dispose of POPs. We can only shift them from place to place. Bacteria won't degrade them. They don't disappear when attached to biodegradable nappies. They can't be neutralised from incinerator smoke stacks. Having killed someone they are free to roam again. **POPs are in the environment and they will stay in the environment – forever.**

Five of the 12 most common POPs are also endocrine-disrupting chemicals (EDCs). The endocrine gland controls hormones, the central nervous system and other key functions of the body. Products can be tested at a few parts per billion for carcinogenic properties, but a few parts per trillion are capable of affecting hormones. Strangely, relatively large doses of EDCs might have no effect, but when tiny doses are administered to rats at a key stage of pregnancy, such as the day on which their hormones trigger limbs to develop, they have a devastating effect

This may explain some strange findings. In the St Lawrence River the population of Beluga whales continued to decline after hunting stopped. It was found that their testes and ovaries were horribly deformed. Similar problems have been found with alligators, polar bears, monkeys, gulls, otters and shellfish. Feminised fish populations are found in nearly every river in Britain.

The chemical industry denies that POPs or EDCs can harm humans ('where are the corpses?') and puts pressure on politicians to allow it to continue unchecked with its hugely profitable, destructive industry. But there is a steady increase in autism, attention deficit hyperactive disorder

(ADHD), dyslexia and uncontrollable aggression, which now affect one in five American children. Thousands of babies in Puerto Rico are experiencing premature breast development. The sperm count of men, globally, has reduced by 50% in the last half century. These symptoms, and many more, are directly related to disruption of the endocrine gland.

Genetically modified crops are not tested for endocrine disruption though there is more reason to suspect that changed genes will be harmful than changed chemicals. Pharmaceuticals also. 'Pharming' these drugs as crops will spread pollen to other crops. Traces of contraceptives and many other synthetic drugs are already found in plants, mammals, birds, fish and drinking water. We will all be ingesting drugs prescribed for others.

The chemical industry, with sales of £400 billion, is conducting a vast uncontrolled experiment on humankind.

Synthetic time bombs are ticking. The United Nations wishes to phase out the use of POPs altogether, against strong opposition from Britain, the US and industry. Sweden is taking the only logical course – in four years it will be illegal to make or use persistent synthetic chemicals, whether or not they are known to cause harm. The WTO, of course, considers this a barrier to trade and may force these poisons on Sweden's citizens – the WTO overrides democracy.

POPs are among the most important ingredients in the vast modern chemical industry. There are more than 100,000 synthetic chemicals on the market. Only 140 have been tested in the last decade. It is only logical that the industry should be required to prove that its chemicals are safe, but their lobby is so well funded it is the consumer that must prove harm before any action is taken – assuming he or she is not already incapacitated or dead.

First generation immigrants to the US have the low-cancer incidence of their native land. Third generation immigrants have the high-cancer incidence of the US.

Our Stolen Future
Theo Colborn et al 1996

Antibiotics

a gift of nature rejected

After 60 years we have thrown away a modern medical miracle.

The first of the five 'kingdoms of life' on earth consisted of bacteria. Some of these are also known as germs because they can invade the human body and cause disease. Bacterial infection, however, can be treated by antibiotics, and the first, penicillin, became available in the 1940s – a medical miracle. There are now 15 types of antibiotic, each of which acts in a different way.

High doses of an antibiotic kill bacteria. But when bacteria are subject to low-level doses, some survive and some die. The ones that survive have a reproductive advantage. By this process the bacteria quickly develop immunity. This is why doctors only prescribe antibiotics when necessary and insist that you complete the course.

Modern surgery was not possible until 1945 when penicillin could kill the most infectious agent, *Staphylococcus Aureus* (SA). By 1947 some SA had become resistant to penicillin. In 1957 methicillin was introduced and methicillin-resistant-SA bacteria (MRSA) developed within two years, making the wards of some hospitals unusable. Now only Vancomysin controls MRSA's worst excesses, but for how long? Vancomysin-resistant bugs have already been detected. Within a few years SA will again become untreatable.

Industrial farming is the worst culprit. Many animals spend miserable lives in cages, without seeing the sun and surrounded in concrete. Farmers feed them antibiotics to make them fat and keep them alive, so bacteria with resistance to antibiotics develop. **Antibiotic resistance in the intestines of farm animals is transferred to bacteria which cause infection in people.**

As usual, the government takes the view that harm has to be proved before any action is taken, otherwise it would be unfair to agribusiness. But the evidence existed in 1998. It is now too late. There are already bacteria resistant to all antibiotics. In 2003, in Britain alone, it is estimated that 5,000 people died from infections resistant to antibiotics. Unbelievably, antibiotic use in intensive farming in Britain is still rising in 2004 – should ministers be held criminally liable?

You may think that plants are not involved. They are now. Most genetically modified crops carry antibiotic-resistance marker genes. Bacteria must be jumping for joy because this low-level presence all over America and on test sites here will allow them to pick up the resistance genes.

When superbugs become common, we face the prospect of untreatable epidemics sweeping the world. Will the first pandemic arise from chicken batteries or from the GM plains of mid-west America?

At the very least, the routine use of antibiotics on farms must be stopped, the precautionary principle must be applied to the approval of drugs, there must be a ban on advertising antibiotics to farmers, and support must be given to organic farming that removes the need for the routine use of antibiotics.

The British Medical Association has called for antibiotic-resistance marker genes to be banned – rather late in the day.

Most of the 800 million chickens consumed in Britain spend short unhappy lives in batteries where they have no chance to develop natural immunity and where parasites and disease spread fast. If the routine abuse of antibiotics is stopped, producers will have to allow the birds healthy lives.

Evolution places us only a step away from apes; they don't think like us but they feel like us. Is it a perversion of Christian theology that allows us to do what we like with them and other animals regardless of what deprivations and suffering we inflict?

Against the Grain
Marc Lappé and
Britt Bailey 1999

Microbes

tougher than humans

Human beings may be clever, but the humble microbe will outlive us.

Let's start with the big picture. It took four billion years for living cells to transform the virgin soup of the atmosphere – a toxic, chaotic mixture of methane, sulphurous compounds, carbon dioxide, and other substances – into conditions that could support life. We must thank the microbes for creating quality out of chaos. Modern civilisation is reversing this. We are digging up everything the microbes 'fixed', we are creating novel materials, plants and gases and disgorging them onto the earth's crust and into the sky. The earth is now running backwards into the chaotic garbage heap from which it started.

But the microbes are still at work. Bacteria, viruses, protozoa, yeasts and algae live in the soil, in water, in the air, on our skin and in our bodies, and are key players in maintaining suitable conditions for life. They recycle nutrients for plants, and in our gut they provide vitamins and aid digestion. Though we can't see them, we use them to make wine, bread, cheese and yogurt.

Microbes have awesome power. A single bacterium can, given the right conditions, take less than a day to multiply to a thousand billion cells. So **a policy of understanding and cooperation, as practiced in organic farming and in much eastern medicine, might be more enlightened** than zapping them whenever they harm our crops or cause us pain.

Our close contact with domestic animals at the dawn of civilisation allowed microbes to jump from them to us, originating many of our 'crowd' diseases: smallpox and tuberculosis came from cattle, the common cold from horses. We developed partial immunity through long contact, but Polynesians and original Americans had virtually no defence when they first came into contact with Europeans carrying these diseases. Pigs have had a bad record: they were responsible for the Asian flu epidemic of 1918-20 which killed 20 million people, more than died in the Great War; and there have been more recent incidents of viruses originating from pigs, particularly in Malaysia; this suggests caution over xenotransplantation, where pigs are used for growing human spare parts.

Other viruses may spread from forests where, until recently, humans have had little contact with wild animals. Aids spread from Zaire in the 1960s but why in modern times and not before? Some scientists think that the Aids epidemic started when a million Africans were used to test a new polio vaccine derived from chimpanzee kidneys in 1957-60, and they urge caution when handling unfamiliar or novel viruses. We are now coming into close contact with a host of unfamiliar microbes as virgin forests are being felled; infections are expected to jump when their natural hosts deplete.

In the 1960s many doctors believed that infectious diseases would soon be conquered, but this hope is now fading and **medicine is increasingly seen as a race to keep ahead of pathogenic microbes.** As soon as cures or new drugs are found, resistant bacteria seem to develop. Many hospitals have had to close wards due to untreatable bacteria or viruses, particularly MRSA. Malaria is spreading north from the tropics. Tuberculosis, which was thought to have been beaten, is coming back, and some strains are already untreatable so that, in New York, the medieval practice of forcible isolation has been reintroduced. People feel vulnerable to diseases that seem to be out of control so new infections like West Nile virus can cause panic; but, when everything in sight is sprayed, the spray may cause more damage than the infection it is supposed to control.

Human presence is the flicker of an eyelid in the timetable of microbes. We cannot assume that humans are somehow above the evolutionary battle and are bound to survive whatever damage we do to other forms of life on earth. A little less arrogance would serve us well.

The Conquest of Disease
Understanding Global Issues 98/2

Genes

and genetic experimentation

Genes are units of heredity – they reproduce themselves from one generation to another. They are fragments of the DNA sequence that have cohesive ends enabling them to be extracted and recombined, hence genetic experimentation is often referred to as 'recombinant DNA technology'.

Forty years ago, molecular scientists dreamed up the wonderfully simplistic 'central dogma' that genes fully account for inherited traits. This gave rise to a multi-billion dollar industry that has made a massive assault on American agriculture. And the Human Genome project, that found the DNA sequences of all the genes in all 23 pairs of chromosomes that exist in every human cell, was heralded as 'the ultimate description of life'.

Instead, the Human Genome project destroyed the scientific basis of genetic engineering. It found that there are far too few genes to account for the complexity of our inherited traits; humans possess even fewer than a blade of grass. An industry that claims to lift agriculture and medicine onto new levels of scientific precision is actually based on a science and a technology in their infancy, at the stage of dropping toys out of the cot to see if they break.

Hype reached the highest political level, and the height of absurdity, with President Clinton describing the genome as "the language in which God created life." Few noticed the sacrilege of suggesting that God could only speak one language.

The human body is made up of cells. An adult has about a hundred thousand billion cells and most cells have a complete set of the genes. The genes turn themselves on or off in different ways in different cells according to their environment in what has been described as a symphony of gene expression. This may explain why chimpanzees, which share 98.5% of our genes, are different from us in almost every detail. A single gene can give rise to multiple proteins so single function genes are a myth. Scientists are undecided whether a genetic disorder is due to the malfunction of a gene, a protein, a chromosome or a cell. There are fewer genes than different proteins in the body and some proteins, called prions, can reproduce themselves without involving DNA at all. **We should be willing to accept how little we truly understand about the secrets of the cell, the fundamental unit of life.**

Biotech companies are playing with just one aspect of life that has interconnections at all levels, and the genetically engineered crops now being grown represent a massive uncontrolled experiment whose outcome is inherently unpredictable. There must be great dangers in overriding patterns of inheritance that are embedded in the natural world through the process of evolution.

Some dangers were appreciated at an early stage. James Watson, joint discoverer of the structure of DNA, issued, with other scientists, an alarming open letter in 1974. Genetic experiments will "result in the creation of novel types of infectious DNA elements" they said "whose biological properties cannot be completely predicted in advance... new DNA elements introduced into E.coli might possibly become widely disseminated among human, bacterial, plant, or animal populations with unpredictable effects." They called for a moratorium on high-risk recombinant DNA experiments. But within a year the potential profits from genetic experimentation became irresistible and many scientists were hooked. In Scotland and Japan, as predicted, there have been incidents where modified E.coli has escaped the laboratory with disastrous results. Dr Mae-Wan Ho suggests that this technology could be the end of humanity. Dare we ignore her?

Changing the genes in every cell of an organism is massively complex. But to modify the egg and sperm before genes divide is relatively simple because you only change a single cell. This is called germ-line therapy. The modified gene will reproduce itself in every cell of the organism as it grows and will be present in future generations. Germ-line therapy can therefore be described as artificial evolution. Whether the gene will stay in the same location in the DNA of second and third generations is disputed and other changes that might occur are not known.

We should question whether we will ever fully understand life and whether it is right for the science to be driven by commercial incentive. History is full of our mistakes. Mistakes with life will have a life of their own.

If the science can avoid too much damage through its early hubris, the manipulation of genes under strictly controlled laboratory conditions may have great benefits. The development of skin grafts and insulin are obvious examples (though the British Diabetic Association has received thousands of letters about unexpected problems apparently caused by GM insulin). Our genetic understanding could surely help sustainable organic farming.

- E.coli is normally harmless. The deadly E.coli 0157:H7 first appeared in the US in 1982 and 9,000 people were affected in Japan in 1992. Last year there were 1,084 cases in the UK.

- Some laboratory rats were exposed to radiation that gave rise to birth defects. The radiation had not changed the genetic code of the offspring. Then the fourth generation of the rats was also found to have the same rate of birth defects as the original parents. The researchers could not understand why the genome had become prone to mutations since the inherited genetic code had not changed. Radiation had destabilised the entire genome of later generations, not just the irradiated sections of the original rat. This indicated that unknown factors come into play with inheritance over several generations that cannot be explained simply by genes.

Genetic Engineering
Dr Mae-Wan Ho 1998

Making New Plants

either GM or organic, which do you prefer?

There is a popular perception that genetic engineering (GE, GM, GMO) is just a development of plant breeding techniques that have been practiced since the dawn of civilisation. No honest scientist would make this claim.

Conventional breeding transfers genetic information between related organisms – members of the same species or, rarely, of closely related genera. Genetic engineering, however, overcomes the barriers that have existed for three billion years of evolution and now transfers genes between unrelated species, genera or kingdoms. For example, a potato may now carry the gene that stops a fish freezing.

Gene transfers aim at certain results, but the process relies on trial and error. Occasionally the transferred gene seems to have the desired effect in the host organism but this may change during the plant's life or in future generations. Several processes are involved in the transfer:

- A **powerful vector** must be used, usually Agrobacterium tumefaciens, a bacterium that causes tumours in plants by inserting DNA from its own genetic code.

- A **promoter** is necessary to overcome a plant's natural resistance to infection. Usually the Cauliflower Mosaic Virus (CMV) is used, a virus that can cause damage to the pancreas, liver and brain of animals that ingest it. It 'turns on' the transferred gene (hyperexpression) but often 'turns on' other genes as well.

- A **marker gene** is added because genetic modification is a haphazard process and the scientist needs to know where the gene has arrived in the host genome. Until recently antibiotic-resistance marker genes were usually used. It has now been found that these genes can be taken up by bacteria in the gut. The British Medical Association says that the use of such genes is 'completely unacceptable'.

- **Random extra genes** get transferred. These are not planned, but strands of unexpected DNA have been found, e.g. in Monsanto soybeans. This DNA may be unstable.

These are some of the ways in which genetic engineering alters plants. Can this really be described as similar to conventional breeding techniques? The biotech industry, with strange logic, claims that genetic engineering is no different from normal plant breeding yet also claims it is a radically new science. US agencies define GM food as 'substantially equivalent' to ordinary food, so consumers are denied labelling.

But Europe was worried that independent testing of GM foods had not been carried out and it imposed a five-year ban on growing GM crops. European regulations have cost US farmers $12 billion in lost trade. European concern has now spread back to the US.

Allergies are a major problem. The National Academy of Sciences, the top US scientific body, warns that **genetically engineered plants may introduce allergens into pollen, which then spreads them in the environment.**

Biotech companies insert toxins into every cell of some plants, our food, as insecticides. The toxins are also released into the ground where they kill susceptible insect larvae and degrade the soil. Low-level toxins in the entire cellular make-up of crops provide ideal conditions for resistance to develop in weeds, insects and bacteria. So dangerous compounds like paraquat and atrazine are being re-introduced to outsmart the pests, though they in turn will become ineffective. In most GM crops the use of herbicides and pesticides is increasing, often just before harvest, so the amount of residues (POPs and EDCs) left on food is also increasing.

Now for the really scary stuff: 'horizontal gene transfer'. Genes are units of heredity – part of the magic that shapes future generations. They go 'vertically' from plant to seed, parent to baby. **But Harvard University and others have found that modified genes also move 'horizontally' from plants to bacteria.** They can move from food to the bacteria in our gut and breach the lining of the womb; we are warned that baby food should not contain GMOs, and it is wise for an expectant mother to avoid GM foods.

Pollen can travel four miles. Draw this circle around an organic or a GM farm and there is no space for the other. Already a farmer with land near a GM plot has been denied the right to grow organic food. **The public wants organic food and there is zero demand for GM food. We can have either one or the other. Not both.**

GM foods have been consumed in the US for seven years without harm, they say. But during this period food-derived illnesses have doubled. In California the number of children with autism has doubled in the last four years. The sperm count of men is steadily reducing. Allergies have greatly increased. But no one knows if this is consequence or coincidence because no monitoring of the long-term clinical or biochemical effects of GM has been done in Britain or the US. The EPA warns that many effects, like cancer and damage to the immune system, could take many years to show.

There are regulations to protect food for humans but are they effective? StarLink corn was approved only for cattle because it contained an allergenic protein. It escaped from animal feed contaminating half the US maize supply and causing allergies from Canada to Japan.

In 2000, researchers from Berkeley found GM contamination in native Mexican corn as well as indications that this transgenic DNA was not stable. The significance was demonstrated by the ferocity of the biotech industry's attacks, not on the research, which had been reproduced and confirmed by the Mexican authorities, but on the researchers. Publication endangered a $50 million grant from Novartis to their university, so the researchers earned the hostility of fellow scientists.

In Britain, the first research into the health effects of GM was so badly handled that it shattered public confidence in the probity of government and its scientific advisers. The unease increased as details emerged. According to four witnesses at the Rowett Institute in Scotland, telephone calls, first from Monsanto to President Clinton, then from Clinton to Tony Blair, then from Blair to the Institute, stopped this key project. Conspiracy theory? But what else might explain subsequent events?

Dr Arpad Pusztai, one of the world's leading experts on plant lectins with 35 years of lab experience, in a project won in competition with 28 other teams, had found that the small intestine, pancreas and brain of rats fed on a GM diet developed differently from the control group. "I believe that this technology can be made to work for us," he said in a short interview on television in 1998 but "it is unfair to use our fellow citizens as guinea pigs, we have to find guinea pigs in the laboratory." The head of the Institute commented on "how well Arpad had answered the questions" and "a range of carefully controlled studies underlie the basis of Dr Pusztai's concerns." The next day Pusztai was told to hand over his data, all GM work was stopped, the team was dispersed and he was threatened with legal action if he spoke to the press. He was banned from his laboratory and his phone calls and emails were diverted. Later the Royal Society, Britain's leading scientific body, was consulted by the government and rushed out a condemnation of his work without obtaining the final report. Then his data were stolen from both his home and the Institute (what burglar would be interested in these?) His work had been peer reviewed six times before being published in The Lancet (whose editor was threatened with loss of pension), well received at a scientific conference and backed by 30 international scientists.

When research is contested, the scientific method is to reproduce it. In this instance, attempts were made to rubbish the 1995-98 study but not to repeat it. The public became acutely aware of the difference between science and commercial science. And confidence in pronouncements on GM by government scientists and the Royal Society plummeted.

The three-year trial of GM crops showed that GM Liberty maize caused marginally less damage to wildlife than conventional maize. But atrazine, a dangerous and banned chemical, had been used. This rendered the test meaningless but has not deterred the government.

In 2003 the British government asked the public if it wanted GM food. 80% said 'no.' Over half said never. It also set up focus groups, citizens' juries, of randomly selected people with no allegiances. As they learned more about it their opinion changed from neutral to anti, in particular that "no one knows enough about the long-term effects on human health." Will it listen?

Lord David Sainsbury, a food industrialist with large interests in plant genetics, is responsible for national policy on GM crops. He has given over £11m to the Labour Party. "Suspicious minds looked at a 300% increase in the government grant to the Sainsbury Laboratory [which researches GM crops] and pondered whether this might be linked to the fact that Lord Sainsbury is the science minister." (*The Times* April 2002)

Atrazine is a horror chemical that disrupts hormones and gets into aquifers. GM Liberty Maize allowed US farmers to stop using it. After a few years weeds developed resistance and GM Liberty Atz is now used – maize with atrazine in every cell.

Percy Schmeiser had bred oilseed rape on his Saskatchewan farm for 50 years and was looking forward to retirement. He noticed some GM canola 'volunteers' (left from previous crops) from a neighbour near his fields. Monsanto had also noticed. Most of his crops were not affected but 60% in one part were contaminated. He had never bought Monsanto's GM seed. Nevertheless, Monsanto served a lawsuit claiming that he had infringed their patent.

Judge W Andrew MacKay's ruling sent shock waves through the farming community: "the source of RR Canola is really not significant for the issue of infringement" he said. Schmeiser lost $600,000 and contamination has ruined his life's work. "If I went down to Monsanto's headquarters and destroyed some of their plants by cross-pollination I would be thrown into jail." he said, "Why does Monsanto have such a right?" – British farmers, beware!

Don't Worry
Andrew Rowell 2003

Seeds of Doubt
Soil Association 2003

The Terminator

force the poor to buy our seeds

*"The earth is not dying, it is being killed.
And those that are killing it have
names and addresses."*
Utah Phillips

The people we are talking about in this chapter are probably decent family men; they probably go to church and believe in a loving God; they probably follow normal business practice. So why are they feared?

'Terminator' technology was a logical business solution. Rather than paying lawyers to sue farmers for saving and sowing patented seed, the seed could be genetically designed to commit suicide. This reduced its yield, and did not exactly improve humanity's ability to cultivate, but Monsanto's friends in the United States Department of Agriculture (USDA) were happy to help. Let's just quote them.

Monsanto: "Terminator technology will open significant world-wide seed markets to the sale of transgenic technology, for crops in which seed currently is saved and used in subsequent plantings."

United States government spokesman, Willard Phelps: "Terminator technology's primary function is to increase the value of proprietary seed owned by US seed companies and to open up new markets in second and third world countries."

Melvin J Oliver, US Department of Agriculture scientist, a government not a company man, explains: "Our mission is to protect US agriculture and to make us competitive in the face of foreign competition. Without this there is no way of protecting the patented seed technology."

After intense worldwide hostility, Monsanto agreed to delay marketing terminator seed for further studies on environmental, economic and social effects. They grudgingly admitted, "We need some level of public acceptance to do our business." However, terminator seeds continue to be patented, including one that becomes sterile only after three generations – a farmer can be fooled into thinking he can replant the seed.

Other companies were also turning plant welfare on its head for commercial gain.

- AstraZeneca was developing seed that is sterile unless its own chemicals are applied.

- Novartis was even developing plants whose resistance to viruses and bacteria have been removed.

Sterile plants, plants that die without chemicals, plants that have no resistance to disease – these are among the achievements of bio companies. They claim that patents on are necessary to enable them to continue to invest in this research and to prevent farmers in poor countries benefiting from their advances.

But that is not all; controlling humanity's food source is only a part of Monsanto's ambitions. To quote Bob Shapiro when Chief Executive, "It is truly easy to make a great deal of money dealing with primary needs: food, shelter, clothing."

"What you are seeing," said Robert Farley of Monsanto in 1998 after describing its purchase of seed companies around the world, "is **not just a consolidation of seed companies, it's really a consolidation of the entire food chain.** Since water is as central to food production as seed, Monsanto is now trying to establish its control over water. Monsanto plans to launch a new water business, starting with India and Mexico, since both these countries are facing water shortages. These are the markets that are most relevant to us as a life science company committed to delivering food, health and hope to the world, and in which there are opportunities to create business value."

Monsanto Strategy Paper: "We are enthusiastic about the potential of partnering the World Bank in joint venture projects in developing markets. The Bank is eager to work with Monsanto." Many Indians understand this to mean that Monsanto aims to control the vital resources of the Indian sub-continent, using public finances (the World Bank) to underwrite the investment. Indian agriculture would then be at the mercy of a private company motivated by profit.

Agricultural biotechnology in the hands of corporations is about control, a branch of empire.

- By 2025 the need for water in India will be 50% more than is available. The crisis will be even greater in 35 year's time when the Himalayan glaciers, which supply summer water to the Indus and the Ganges, are gone. The water table in most states in India is dropping at the rate of one yard a year. Will water companies be more interested in thirsty peasants than industry?

- One company, Cargill, controls 80% of global grain distribution. The top ten corporations control: 85% of all pesticides, 60% of all veterinary medicine, 35% of all pharmaceuticals, 32% of all commercial seed.

- The government of Brazil, responding to the will of its people, banned the planting of GM Soya. Monsanto spent $600m in buying Brazilian seed companies and encouraging farmers to smuggle large quantities of GM seed across the border. Monsanto has not been charging royalties. The government was forced to cave in and Brazil is no longer a GM free country.

- Monsanto's New Leaf potato incorporates pesticides in every cell and the potato itself has to be registered as a pesticide.

- In 2002 the massive failure of Bt cotton in India's southern states led to a ban on planting in northern states.

- Astra Zeneca makes tamoxofen, a breast cancer drug. It also makes acetochlor, a pesticide identified as a cause of cancer. This forms a neat business cycle, perhaps suggested by its accountant.

- Monsanto say gene spread is not a problem but also say that terminator crops are necessary to overcome the problem.

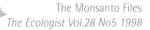

Nature in Balance

survival of the fittest?

The skeletal structure of the Oxford Museum, with a giant dinosaur across its main hall, is where the first debates on the origin of species took place. In a cabinet there are two bean-weevils that are so small they can sit comfortably on a match head but their rate of reproduction is prodigious. Beside them is a glass jar. Dr George McGavin, the curator, says that it would take only about 70 days of unchecked mating of the weevils and their progeny for the jar to be filled with their eggs. If they continued thus they would fill the room in 100 days and the entire internal volume of the earth in a little over 15 months. If this happened they would, of course, have nothing to eat. By winning, they would be on the losing side. Nature, during four billion years, has evolved plenty of checks to stop this happening. If any species is too successful its population may suddenly collapse.

Each species needs a balanced habitat to provide it with food and each species is subject to a balance of predators and microbes. But the balance can be rocked. When a plant or creature from one part of the world is introduced into another it may no longer have the natural restraints that had evolved in its original habitat. Biologists refer to the 10/10 principle: one in 10 alien organisms will thrive in a new environment and one in 10 of those that thrive will become a pest.

There were no rabbits in Australia until a few were deliberately introduced in 1859; they soon spread throughout the continent with disastrous results. A single Japanese Knotweed, planted in a garden near Brighton, escaped into a rubbish tip and has now spread throughout the UK; it is unaffected by pesticides and Swansea has a full-time Knotweed officer who reckons it would cost $15 million to eradicate it from the city (it would return, of course). Mink escaping from farms have threatened the survival of some native species. The gray squirrel has displaced the red squirrel in many countries. The zebra mussel has caused havoc in the Great Lakes of North America. The comb jellyfish has colonised the Black Sea. Water hyacinth has clogged waterways in Africa and India.

Whether the 10/10 principle will apply to genetically modified plants and animals is an open question. Some novel organisms are being deliberately released as trial crops. In laboratories, novel bacteria and viruses are developed as vectors to transfer genes from one species to another. Genes from animals are being introduced into agriculture and human surgery.

But once novel plants, bacteria, viruses or animals are out in the open they have a life of their own and they are no longer in our control. As they are new to nature it is unlikely they will be subject to the constraints that have developed over millions of years.

Seen from space the biosphere seems a fragile skin, as delicate as the bloom on a peach. But humanity is infinitely more fragile. We do not control nature, nature supports us. Nature has evolved in a way that retains a balance. The forests act as the lungs of the world and contain unexplored genetic richness; plants and plankton begin the food chain on land and sea; micro-organisms make the soil fertile and enable creatures to digest food – but it is presumptuous comment on this infinite complexity. Creatures that disturb this balance find themselves rejected.

Where Next
Duncan Poore 2000

Population

more or less

The world population in 2050 will be decided by three billion women. If every second woman decides to have three rather than two children, the population will rise to 27 billion. The best guess is that, on average, women will have 2.1 children, the 'fertility rate', and the population will stabilise. If, however, every second woman decides to have only one child instead of two, the world population will sink to 3.6 billion. Small changes in people's motivation result in huge changes to numbers.

Corporations use the scare of rising numbers to justify risky experiments with chemicals and genes, and politicians justify economic growth as necessary for controlling population.

Stable societies in the past may have understood 'carrying capacity' – the ability of their environment to sustain the desired quality of life over a long period. For example, the early colonisers of America had larger families than their relatives in crowded Europe. But improved agriculture and aid programs released families from this bondage and they felt confident in having more children. Better expectations and reduced infant mortality resulted in the population explosion. We face the paradox that the expectation of food security caused the world population to rise but the number of hungry people is now greater than ever before.

Human population increased very gradually over thousands of years. Then, following the industrial revolution, the rate of growth suddenly shot up, particularly since 1950. Since the 1970s there has been a gradual reduction in the rate of growth in most parts of the world. The usual way of predicting numbers is to guess at fertility rates and assume that, since they have always increased in the past, they will continue to increase in future but will level off in due course.

Demographers also use the technique of fitting a mathematical equation to past trends. This shows a startling outcome. The graph levels off in 20 years' time then drops to pre-industrial levels.

Falling confidence in the economy could provide feedback that reduces parents' perception of their future prospects, thus reducing the fertility rate. And global warming, spread of tropical diseases and increased conflict, point to a higher mortality rate. These trends tend to confirm the mathematical approach. Today, more than 60 countries have fertility rates below replacement level and the rate of growth in other countries is reducing. As their populations get older, rich countries will compete for immigrants of working age from poor countries.

The surge of population during the last century may have been a temporary phenomenon brought on by access to the cheap energy on which almost all our technology depends. The graph of population numbers may end up resembling the bell shaped graph followed by the extraction of oil (p44). In due course the human population may return to a level that is within the carrying capacity of the world.

Italy and Norway

It is ironic that Bianca in Catholic Italy has just 1.2 children, which signals a crash from 56 to 8 million Italians this century; whereas Astrid in Norway has 1.8 children. Why? Bianca is well educated and has prospects but there is poor state childcare provision and Italian men are not renowned for helping in the home. Astrid is just as keen to pursue a career but the government helps mothers to juggle family and work, about half the jobs held by women are part-time, crèches are universal, paid parental leave lasts for a year and her husband is better house-trained, so the population is stable.

World fertility rate:

1950   5.0 children per woman.
Today   2.7 children per woman.

Population Politics
Virginia Abernethy 1999

Patenting Life

wait a minute! who made it?

Only 'commerce' could think of allowing life forms to be privately owned. An African tribal-doctor might wish to keep his remedies secret but no one would deny others the chance to emulate him. Indians know trees by their medicinal properties, and the idea that anyone should pay a fee for using these properties is inconceivable. It has been accepted that anyone in the world can use the resources of nature – until 20 years ago.

It happened in the US. A genetically engineered micro-organism, designed to consume oil spills, provided the test case. The Patents and Trademark Office (PTO) rightly rejected the application, arguing that living things could not be patented under US law. But at appeal the patent was allowed by a narrow majority on the basis that the microorganism was "more akin to inanimate chemical compositions than to horses and honeybees." The PTO, still believing that patenting life forms was wrong, appealed to the Supreme Court, which upheld the patent in 1980. But four of the nine judges strongly opposed it and it was nearly rejected.

Then in 1987 the PTO did an astonishing about-turn. It issued a ruling that all genetically engineered living organisms can be patented – including human genes, cell-lines, tissues, organs, and even genetically altered human embryos and fetuses. This ruling opened the floodgates.

Patented things have to be 'novel, non-obvious and useful.' No one has ever argued that oxygen or helium, for example, however non-obvious and however useful, can be patented just because a chemist has isolated, classified, and described their properties. These elements are not novel; they exist in nature. But with total lack of consistency the PTO now holds that anyone can claim a human invention simply by isolating and classifying a gene's properties and purposes, even though these are not novel but pre-exist in nature. No molecular biologist has ever created a gene, cell, tissue, organ, or organism *de novo*.

The first mammal to be patented was a mouse with human genes. The team that created Dolly the sheep applied for a broad patent to cover all cloned animals. Then, a businessman, John Moore, received hospital treatment for a rare form of cancer; later he found that the University of Los Angeles had patented his body parts and licensed them to a pharmaceutical company at a value of $3 billion; the California Supreme Court ruled that Moore had no rights over his own body tissues. A broad patent gives Briocyte worldwide ownership of all human blood cells from the umbilical cord of babies for pharmaceutical purposes, even though the company has only isolated and described the blood cells.

Broad patents have caused furore. Patenting of the properties of the Neem tree and Basmati rice by US companies has provoked violent anger throughout India. A US professor failed in his attempt to patent turmeric for medicinal purposes but it cost India $500,000 to fight the case. India will not fight Monsanto's patent on the wheat used for centuries to make chapatis, it can't afford to fight every ludicrous case – financial might, not right, wins – but don't be surprised when yet more corporate US property is trashed by angry farmers in India. Papua was furious when the US government patented cell lines from its citizens. The arrogance of this new colonialism is breathtaking. Patents take no account of the transformation of wild grasses, tubers etc. into crops by indigenous people over millennia. They literally allow western companies to hijack knowledge that has been used by all and charge others for using it. But poor nations fear sanctions if they do not adopt US practice.

The World took a wrong turning in America 23 years ago. Might India declare, unilaterally, that the fundamental elements of life are global commons and ought never to be up for sale to private interests at any price? All life knowledge, at present in private hands, would then be freely available on the sub-continent. Perhaps India would become the powerhouse of the life sciences because of this freedom

Commercial Eugenics

an alternative future for the poor

Economic inequality has become extreme. But redistribution of wealth is extremely unpopular among the rich who wield power. They may decide instead to solve humanity's biggest problem by taking inequality into new spheres.

Our mental capacity evolved to meet the needs of hunter-gatherers and is built into our makeup. Even isolated tribal people, given the right training, can use the Internet. So, by imagining hunter-gatherer society, some believe, we can begin to understand some human oddities – man is promiscuous and woman coy because that helps his genes to multiply and hers to use their annual chance to obtain quality. It is a compulsive game that you play according to your interests.

A sociologist asks why we are able to co-operate well in groups up to 150 but are often hopeless at larger scale decision-making. An art historian asks why we like landscape paintings that have an edge-of-forest feel. Evolutionary psychology is a surprisingly static cause-and-effect type of theory.

Scientists have latched onto the popular cause-and-effect concept because it captures the imagination and helps to release funds. Almost daily, scientists claim to find genes for this and that: a gene for inherited disease, for alcoholism, for aggression, for depression, for dyslexia . . .

Finding and neutralising the gene for Down's syndrome would be one of the great achievements of medicine. If air traffic controllers could be screened for genetic pre-disposition to black out it would surely be our duty to protect the public. If we could find correlation between a gene and aggressive behaviour perhaps we could reduce crime. In California genetic scans are already used in the sentencing process to determine whether a convicted criminal is likely to re-offend.

Insurance companies are bound to ask for genetic screening or at least for us to declare any tests that show genetic pre-dispositions. Employers will want to check that their investment in trainees is unlikely to be wasted. The billionaire will want to ensure that his progeny are tall, intelligent and sociable – all traits which, it is claimed, can be enhanced by genetic modification. We are at an early stage of the science but if these techniques become possible they are bound to be adopted.

Instead of having a genetic make-up that was developed for hunter-gatherers and is ill adapted to modern society, we can now change our genes to suit our present needs, they say. In our market-driven society this will no doubt be achieved through personal and commercial incentives.

Molecular Biologist Lee Silver of Princeton University regards himself as one of the scientists blazing a trail to a future containing the Gene-Rich and the Naturals. The Gene-Rich, offspring of today's super-rich, will be about 10% of the population, enhanced with synthetic genes and having the life-span of Methuselah. The Gene-Rich will become the rulers of society – businessmen, musicians, artists, athletes and scientists. "With the passage of time," Lee Silver predicts, "the genetic distance will become greater and greater, and there will be little movement up from the Natural to the Gene-Rich class. Naturals will work as low-paid service providers or as labourers" – no doubt with good television to divert them. "Gene-Rich humans and Natural humans will be entirely separate species with no ability to cross-breed and with as much romantic interest in each other as a current human would have for a chimpanzee."

The higher species may treat us as we treat lesser species. A humane cull may be necessary to tackle one of our biggest problems – the adverse environmental effects of excessive numbers.

The Biotech Century
Jeremy Rifkin 1998

Nanotechnology

success might be the worst-case scenario

Deconstruct a potato atom by atom, store the information on a computer, broadcast it to the other side of the world where they can feed dust into a few trillion nano-assemblers and, hey presto, they reconstruct the potato. That may be an extreme description of what could be the defining technology of the coming century.

Nanotechnology aims to manipulate atoms. At this scale air and rock, life and non-life, mind and matter, are all assemblies of atoms arranged in different ways. It is the ultimate 'convergence' science that spans all academic disciplines from physics to biology to health to cognitive neuroscience. A lay person can't hope to understand the science, but it sounds exciting: "it will solve humanity's material needs"; "we can all have a better quality of life without having to work"; "electricity will be too cheap to meter" (we have heard that one before); "neurons could be re-engineered so that our minds talk directly to computers or artificial limbs"; "fine-tuning our metabolism could stop ageing"; "computer networks could be merged with biological networks to develop surveillance systems"; "viruses could be re-engineered to act as weapons.". These are some of the longer-term claims. A shorter-term prediction recorded by *The Economist* may be a more realistic reason for the hype: "It will be a trillion-dollar business in ten years time."

For 200 years new sciences have transformed human life and capabilities so we are always optimistic that the next science will solve the problems left by previous ones – and anyone who questions an exciting new science is dismissed by politicians as a Luddite. But the fruits of the tree of knowledge seem to suffer from a curse.

The Industrial Revolution has given developed countries undreamed of riches but it also started the process of global warming. Nuclear science threatens global holocaust. Antibiotics have been only a temporary miracle. Persistent synthetic chemicals have worked their way up the food chain and affect reproduction and the central nervous system. So new sciences have both good and bad aspects and the more powerful the science the more extreme the consequences.

We are now reaching out for the fruits of the tree of life. The jury on genetic science is still out but it is controlled by corporations for profit so the downside will be concealed. Nanotechnology may be the most powerful technology that has ever existed, with wonderful potential. But ultra-fine particles (UFPs), for example, of a size that is extremely rare in nature, can penetrate skin and alveolar membranes, leaving the body wide open to toxic effects – and UFPs are already being used in a wide range of applications from drug delivery to sun creams. A particularly jolly warning by none other than Bill Joy, managing director of Sun Microsystems, is that out-of-control self-replicating nanobots might reduce global ecosystems to grey goo in a matter of days.

Let's hope that this is just imaginative science fiction.

Sciences develop in phases. First excitement. Then hard sell. Then reality. Nanotechnology is at the beginning of the second phase.

Unfortunately, the greatest possible success for the science could be the worst-case scenario for society. If the technology lives up to its promises, if human effort is replaced once and for all, if our life can be spent pursuing art, literature and video games, if danger has to be artificially created to give us thrills, then human nature changes. Proponents of nanotechnology talk cheerfully about a post-human future. But human meaning is produced by human effort and we may be deprived of the life we need to live.

NBIC. 'Nano-Bio-Info-Cogno' is a project that has received the biggest research grant since the space programme in the US. It will use nanoscience for brain implants, genetic modification, pharmaceuticals, nuclear weaponry, intelligent uniforms etc., in a strategic bid to extend US commercial and military dominance.

Understanding Nature

and re-designing life

Our understanding of the world around us is determined, to a great extent, by the culture in which we live.

St Thomas Aquinas saw the natural world as a Great Chain, a myriad of plants and animals in a descending hierarchy of importance. For him nature required dependent relationships and obligations among creatures that God had created. Diversity and inequality guaranteed the orderly working of the system. His portrayal of nature reflected the hierarchical structure of the medieval society in which he lived.

Later, Darwin's portrayal of nature also reflected the society in which he lived. The capitalist marketplace was competitive, where only the fittest survived and his theories about plants, animals or man reflected this. As with the perfecting of machines, evolution in nature produced better and better models. His theory precisely matched Adam Smith's 'invisible hand' that enabled acts of individual selfishness to result in general well being. The intrinsic value of each living thing in the medieval paradigm was replaced by mere utility value. Individual, clan, village and town structures, in which people could choose how they wish to live and what they wish to protect, gave way to types, categories and the dehumanisation of politics. This allowed dictators or political cliques to act out theories in which people – as machines or competing economic units – could be manipulated to suit a particular social theory. It led directly to communism, to the eugenic experiments of the last century and to market fundamentalism.

Nature is now being cast in the image of the computer and information science. Creatures are no longer birds and bees, foxes and hens, but bundles of genetic information with no sacred boundaries between species. In commerce, new groups of companies are emerging with shared relationships within complex embedded networks that are able to respond quickly to fast-changing flows of information. A generation brought up in a computerised society can accept information as a basis for understanding nature. It reassures us that the infinite and chaotic complexities and multi-faceted expansions of all our activities, our ever-shifting life-styles, and our experimentation with genes, are in harmony with the evolutionary processes of nature. Thus we avoid feeling confused and threatened.

In the 1940s Norbert Wiener pioneered the concept that "all living things are really patterns that perpetuate themselves. A pattern is a message and may be transmitted as a message; the fact that we cannot telegraph the pattern of a man from one place to another seems to be due to technical difficulties." This is a concept that will be familiar to viewers of Star Trek.

The ability to handle information, rather than to develop knowledge or wisdom, is typical of modern life: today's understanding gives way to tomorrow's; we must be continually open to new scenarios; through drugs and plastic surgery we can reinvent ourselves; life and work are games to be played.

Molecular biologists no longer talk of laws of nature or objective reality, but of 'scenarios', 'models', 'creative possibilities' – this is the language of architects or artists. Those at the cutting edge see their ability to handle almost unlimited information through computers (soon to be living DNA computers) as a natural extension of evolution. Evolution has now passed into their hands (they say 'into humanity's hands' but who else has the ability except molecular biologists?) **Molecular biologists are the artists of new forms of life; they will modify and design future generations.** In other words they are the invisible hand of Darwin's natural selection or the God of St. Thomas Aquinas.

But a new consciousness is emerging that approaches the world we share with other cultures, other creatures and a myriad of life forms, with awe and reverence.

Intuition

common sense, imagination and morality

Science is largely responsible for our progress and prosperity, and it is natural to look first to scientists for the answers to difficult questions.

But science, almost by definition, is reductionist – it looks at the simple constituents of complex things. Science can improve crop yields but not get the additional food to hungry mouths. Scientists have made no secret of their ignorance about the political effects of nuclear energy, and these effects have proved more important than the science itself. Governments like to claim scientific support partly because it allows them to make decisions within a cabal of experts, bureaucrats and corporate managers, hidden from the public behind obscure language. But recent events suggest that we should give more weight to intuition, imagination, common sense and morality.

💡 **Intuition** might have prevented the British turning cows into cannibals – they would have avoided BSE, cattle would have suffered less, and they would have saved $8 billion.

💡 **Imagination** could show that clear labelling of content and origin would enable epidemiologists to trace what is happening in a complex food system, and help people to make informed decisions on what they wish to buy.

💡 **Common sense** would tell us that a centralised food system is dangerous – without such a system two gallons of transformer oil would not have destroyed Belgium's entire food economy in 1999. Common sense surely tells us that planting crops that are genetically new to nature, on the basis of "let's see what happens," could be rather like releasing rats to see whether or not they spread bubonic plague. Common sense tells us that the cost of coal, oil, gas and water should reflect depletion and contribution to climate change, not just the cost of extraction.

Morality tells us not to keep chickens in such crowded conditions that they can't walk, live only six weeks and are then shackled upside down to a conveyor belt before being killed. Without this cruelty we would not have salmonella. Morality tells us to ban BST hormone treatment because it causes acute suffering to cows, let alone the suffering it might cause humans. Morality tells us not to participate in inhuman trading practices. Morality, eventually, told us to stop slavery.

When intuition, imagination, common sense or morality – let alone science – suggest that a new policy, product or procedure is suspect, **it should be the responsibility of the promoter to prove** **that the objections are unfounded.** This is the 'precautionary principle.' Our government and the World Trade Organisation act on the basis that no restriction must be allowed until conclusive evidence shows harm. By then the damage is done.

Some countries use citizen's juries, chosen at random, who are presented with some technical background and a host of expert and lay views as to whether a certain area of research is worth pursuing. The citizens' jury then comes to a verdict as to whether the research seems reasonable and fair by criteria that they themselves develop. Both scientists and political theorists have been surprised and impressed by the results.

"Failing to understand the consequences of our inventions… seems to be a common fault of scientists and technologists. We are being propelled into the new century with no plan, no control and no brake."
Bill Joy
Chief scientist, Sun Microsystems

Two Japanese Farmers

more with less – a fascinating tale

Weeding rice paddy-fields is very labour intensive so Japanese farmers eagerly adopted the chemical approach, even though it did not improve on the high yield of traditional Japanese methods. Only a few farmers held back from the Agrichemical Revolution.

The Furunos are a Japanese farming couple who do not use chemicals. Their system uses ducklings to fertilise the fields and eat the weeds. The rice has a very high yield and they get four different harvests: rice, fish (roach), eggs and ducks. In spite of a life spent perfecting the system they are happy for it to be adopted by anyone. "Financial success is not important." They say, **"We did not patent the method, we just want it to be widely adopted."** Ten thousand farmers now use the method in Japan and it is spreading throughout South-East Asia.

Masanobu Fukuoka inherited a farm from his father. He claims to be lazy. "If things grow in the wild on their own, why does one have to do so much hard work?" he would ask. So in a short time he had destroyed his father's orange orchard and was having similar success with the rice. But he persisted with his unusual convictions and over the years developed a system of 'do nothing' farming. He does not flood his rice fields, he does not weed them, he does not dig or plough and, above all, he does not use any chemicals. Yet his crops are resistant to pests, yield as much as traditional or chemical rice growing, and require much less work.

But the system requires careful management of crops and is related to a particular location. The farmer needs to know the microclimate and be observant. In the autumn he sows rice, clover and winter barley and covers them with straw. The barley grows immediately and is harvested in May and its straw scattered on the fields. The spring monsoon weakens the weeds and allows the rice to grow through the ground cover. Nothing more is done until the rice is harvested in October. Over the years the soil has got richer and richer with no ploughing, without taking away the straw, and with no addition of manure or fertilisers. "This is a balanced rice field ecosystem," he says "Insect and plant communities maintain a stable relationship here. It is not uncommon for a plant disease to sweep through the area, leaving the crops in these fields unaffected."

He has a similar approach to his restored orchard, harvesting a great variety of vegetables under the trees without cultivation but with a lot of care. And he has the time to be a philosopher.

Both farmers achieve yields that could make Japan self-sufficient in food, but the government persists in supporting chemical methods using alien seed.

"Because the world is moving with such furious energy in the opposite direction," Fukuoka-sen says, "it may appear that I have fallen behind the times, but I firmly believe that the path I have been following is the most sensible one."

The One Straw Revolution
Masanobu Fukuoka 1992

Mental Equipment

reality beyond our grasp

Our brains did not appear suddenly from nowhere; they evolved in the same way that other parts of our bodies evolved. Gradually, over hundreds of thousands of years before settled civilisation, those with greater abilities supplanted others. So our mental equipment is appropriate for specific needs and is related to just five senses. It is not an abstract intelligence designed to comprehend all of existence, however much we use this equipment to understand and manipulate the world around us. It has limitations.

To appreciate the implications you only have to imagine a group that lacks one of the five senses, a group that has been blind from birth, discussing sight. They have heard people talk about colour, about clouds, about mist, about distance and about beauty. How would they discuss these concepts among themselves? Some might say it is all a myth and deny that sight exists; some might be acutely frustrated that they can't quite grasp the idea; some might develop a form of words and bully others to accept their definition and others might be more tentative and try to feel their way into an understanding.

If our cognitive equipment evolved to meet the needs of hunter-gatherers it is not surprising that some aspects of reality are simply beyond our grasp, just as a dog picks up only part of your meaning: "blah blah blah fido blah blah." But we do seem to sense further reality through a dark distorting glass. Our vague perceptions are the stuff of mystics, poets, musicians and painters. Religions have tried to tie these realities down into concepts and words.

Even scientists describe things that fall beyond comprehension. Newtonian physics and Cartesian geometry made sense to our five senses. No longer. Matter is now known to be a mass of energy, more like a web of interpenetrating vibrations than like solid building blocks. Particles of energy are connected to each other in mysterious ways, seemingly unlimited by space and time. An experiment is changed by being viewed. Scientists now even suggest that 'string', with ten dimensions and a whole world of magnitude below the size of molecules, could give clues for understanding the infinite vastness of an expanding universe. All this points to connections at a far deeper level than we will ever fully comprehend.

If there were creatures whose cognitive equipment had evolved beyond ours, they might be amused at the way we describe concepts that are mysterious to us but clear and obvious to them. But they might also be alarmed that our technology allows us to play with things whose full interconnectedness we can't possibly appreciate – they might see us wandering towards the precipice and be shouting **"for God's sake STOP!"**

I, the fiery light of divine wisdom,
I ignite the beauty of the plains,
I sparkle the waters.
I burn the sun and the moon and the stars,
With wisdom I order all rightly.
I adorn all the earth.
I am the breeze that nurtures all things green.
I am the rain coming from the dew
That causes the grasses to laugh
With the joy of life.
I call forth tears, the aroma of holy work.
I am the yearning for good.

Hildegard of Bingen
1098–1179

How the Mind Works
Stephen Pinker 1997

References

The Little Earth Book
Visit our website at **www.littleearth.co.uk** for links.

General sources
Global Environment Outlook (GEO 2000 and annual)
UN Environment Programme annual reports
UN Development Programme annual reports
Royal Commission on Environmental Pollution reports
Worldwatch Institute reports
Friends of the Earth: Tomorrow's World

Organisations
Actionaid: www.actionaid.org.uk
Alliance for America: www.allianceforamerica.org
Alliance for Democracy
ASPO The Association for the Study of Peak Oil:
    www.energiekrise.de and: www.asponews.org
Bank of England: www.bankofengland.co.uk
BBC science: http://bbc.co.uk/science
Best Foot Forward: http://bestfootforward.com
Bradford Peace Studies: www.brad.ac.uk/acad/peace
Campaign Against the Arms Trade: www.caat.org.uk
CAT Centre for Alternative Technology
Center for Concern: www.coc.org
Citizens' Income Trust: www.citizensincome.org

CNES Center for Network on Essential Services:
    www.servicesforall.org
Die Off: www.dieoff.org
Disinformation (alternative news and underground
    culture): www.disinfo.com
Earth Council: www.ecouncil.ac.cr
Earth Policy Institute: www.earth-policy.org
Ecologist: www.theecologist.org
FEASTA. The Foundation for the Economics of
    Sustainability: www.feasta.org
Footprint: www.iclei.org
Friends of the Earth: www.foe.co.uk
GCI: Global Commons Institute: www.gci.org.uk
Globe Post: www.travelselect.com
Going for Green: www.goingforgreen.org.uk
Green Party: www.greenparty.org.uk
Greenpeace: www.greenpeace.org
INES, issues of global responsibility:
    www.inesglobal.org
ITDG Intermediate Technology Development Group:
    www.itdg.org
Jefferson Center (citizens juries):
    www.jefferson-center.org.
Land Value Tax Campaign: www.landvaluetax.org
Move On (democracy in action): www.moveon.org

Met Office Hadley Centre: www.met-office.gov.uk
New Internationalist. www.newint.org
New Scientist. www.newscientist.com
Mother Jones magazine. www.motherjones.com
Nature Research Journal: www.nature.com
New Economics Foundation: www.neweconomics.org
New Internationalist: www.newint.org
New Scientist: www.newscientist.com
ORG. Oxford Research Group (peace studies)
    www.oxfordresearchgroup.org.uk
Permaculture: www.permaculture.co.uk
Pew Center on Climate Change: www.pewclimate.org
Positive News: www.positivenews.org.uk
Preparing for Peace (essays suggesting that war is no
    longer an option): www.preparingforpeace.org
Progress Report: www.progress.org
Public Citizen: www.citizen.org.
Rachel's Environment and Health Weekly:
    www.rachel.org
Rio + 10 (Johannesburg): www.rio-plus-10.org
RSPB: www.rspb.org.uk
Royal Commission on Environmental Pollution. 22nd
    report (UK official scientific report on climate
    change): www.rcep.org.uk
Scientific American: www.sciam.com
Sky Trust, (sky a global common)
    www.skytrust.cfed.org.
Soil Association: www.soilassociation.org
State of the World, Worldwatch Institute (annual)
Survival. (indigenous): www.survival-international.org

Sustainable Society Directory:
    www.sustainable-society.co.uk
TNS The Natural Step: www.naturalstep.org.
Turning Point Project: www.turnpoint.org
UCS. Union of Concerned Scientists: www.ucsusa.org
UNDP Human Development Reports (annual):
    www.undp.org
UNEP Global Environment Outlook: www.unep.org
US Global Change Research Program: www.gcrio.org
US National Academy of Sciences: www.nas.edu
US National Oceanic and Atmospheric Administration:
    www.noaa.gov
Vostok ice core data: http://cdiac.esd.ornl.gov
WDM World Development Movement: www.wdm.org.uk
WTO (spin-free): www.gatt.org/trastat_e.html
WWF. www.worldwildlife.org
Yes magazine: www.yesmagazine.org
Z Communication (articles+Chomsky): www.zmag.org

Prominent organisations committed to the rape of the
planet (along with the World Bank, IMF, WTO:
The Adam Smith Institute: www.adamsmith.org
the Institute of Economic Affairs: www.iea.org.uk
Competitive Enterprise Institute (US): www.cei.org
George C Marshall Institute (US): www.marshall.org
Most British MPs accept the science of climate change
but take no effective action. Various US Senators loudly
deny the science of climate change: vice-president Dick
Cheney, James Inhofe (chair of Senate committee on
environment), Larry Craig, Craig Thomas.

Notes on some chapters

• **Introduction** • Full text of the Scientists' Warning: www.ucsusa.org.

• **Don't Predict** • The principles are derived from the four 'System Conditions' of *The Natural Step*, but see the book for a full description. The conditions were developed by the oncologist Dr Karl-Henrik Robèrt and achieved consensus among scientists in Sweden. They provide a working definition for 'upstream' action on sustainability. Most other definitions, such as Brundtland, have little practical application for development • *Playing Safe - Science and the Environment* by Jonathon Porritt

• **Ozone** • in 2002 there was an encouraging reduction of the ozone hole but in 2003 it was larger than ever.

• **Water** • for the disastrous effect of the current construction of the Narmada dam in India see *The Cost of Living* by Arundhati Roy.

• **Ecological Footprints** • *The Ecological Footprint theory* was developed by Wackernagel & Rees. For a fuller discussion of Kerala see *The Growth Illusion* by Douthwaite and *Hope Human and Wild* by Bill McKibben. Also based on personal experience • China warning is by Klaus Topfer of UNEP • *Monitoring the Environment* ed. by Bryan Cartledge (with diverse viewpoints) • *The Earth Transformed - an Introduction to Human Impacts on the Environment* by Andrew Goudie and Heather Viles • *Our Final Century - Will the Human Race Survive the twenty-First Century?* by Martin Rees, *Astronomer Royal* (readable and pleasantly detached, like Humpty on a wall)

• **Atmospheric Carbon** • *US National Security Strategy* Ch.6 p20 makes climate change a security issue. However the Bush administration has the most destructive environmental record of any and it has even censored the climate section of the EPA's annual scientific report • *Abrupt Climate Change - Inevitable Surprises* by US NAS 2001 • PEW Center: "warming in the U.S is expected to be higher than elsewhere… sea-level rise will gradually inundate coastal areas, increased risk of droughts and floods, threats to biodiversity and a number of potential challenges for public health. We must fundamentally transform the way we power our global economy." • For the Permian extinctions see *When Life Nearly Died - the Greatest Mass Extinction of All Time* by Michael J Benton 2003 • see *Die Off* article on Climate Change • *The Breathing Planet - a scientific guide*, ed. by John Gribbin

• **Europe Cooling** • Potsdam Institute prepared computer model of Atlantic currents • Scottish Executive's Marine Lab. Aberdeen published measurements of reducing salinity "consistent with models showing the stopping of the pump and the conveyor belt" • Fisheries Lab. of the Faroes records increasing temperature of pump water • Bergen University reported Greenland-Norway current into reverse.

• **Rio and Kyoto** • There is well funded denial of global warming by vested interests, originally led by the discredited Global Climate Coalition and now by Western Fuels Inc., an organisation representing the coal industry.

• **Contraction & Convergence** • UK government has

acknowledged the RCEP recommendation. Margaret Beckett of DEFRA, strangely, claims that least developed countries reject C&C when the reverse is the case, they are among its strongest supporters (this is probably an excuse for inaction, made without bothering to check the facts)

• **DTQs** • see also the Sky Trust in the US, which would sell a gradually reducing number of carbon emission permits and divide the income equally among all citizens. Its principles are: 1/ The sky belongs to all of us equally. 2/ The sky does not belong to corporations or the government. 3/ Pollution must be limited to what the sky can safely absorb. 4/ Once limits are set, companies should pay for pollution permits. 5/ The money they pay should go into a trust. 6/ The trust should pay equal dividends to all citizens

• See chapter on Citizens' Income.

• **Future of Oil** • *Hubbert's Peak* by Kenneth S Deffeyes • ASPO newsletters for monthly independent updated assessment of oil depletion • *New Rulers of the World* by John Pilger 2000 • Seizure of Saudi oilfields and comments on Saudi investments in the US, see Report to the Pentagon by the Rank think-tank • *Die Off* article on Oil Depletion • *Before the Wells Run Dry* by Feasta 2003.

• **Weapons of War** • *Resource Wars* by Michael T Klare • *Guns, Germs and Steel* by Jared Diamond • *Straw Dogs* by John Gray 2002 • *The Invention of Peace & the Reinvention of War* by Michael Howard

• **Tools for Peace** • *Preparing for Peace* lectures • examples taken from *War Prevention Works* by Dylan Mathews Oxford Research Group 2001 • *The Peace Book - 108 simple ways to create a more peaceful world* by Louise Diamond 2001 • *People, Peace and Power - Conflict Transformation in Action* by Diana Francis

• **Inequality** • diagram from *UNDP Human Development Report* 1999 • US prison population: *Washington Post* February 2000 • US health cover: *The Economist* 20 January 2001 • figures on poverty: *Unicef Report* September 2001 • *Understanding Capitalism* by Douglas Dowd

• **Interest-free Banking** • *Time Banks - No More Throw-Away People* by Edgar S Cahn 2000 • *Inclusive Economics - Gandhian Method and Contemporary Policy* by Narendar Pani

• **Wörgl** • *After the Black Death* by George Huppert 1986 • The "Chiemgauer" is a voucher local currency system started in Germany in 2002 and attracting much attention from other communities, see www.Chiemgauer-regional.de • *Funny Money* by David Boyle • *The Social Meaning of Money* by Kenneth O Doyle

• **Global Eco-Currency** • Douthwaite's strategy is selected because it relates the monetary system to environmental and societal needs with great clarity • *Rethinking Bretton Woods: Center for Concern* factsheet • *Beyond Globalization* by Hazel Henderson • *Sustainable Economics:* monthly newsletter from the Green Party • *Radical Economics* newsletter from the New Economics Foundation

• **Citizens' Income** • see: www.progress.org • *Economic Justice for All* by Michael Murray 1997 • BIEN Basic Income Network Europe. ww.bien.be • The Tragedy of the Commons - destroyed by unregulated use. Under market fundamentalism global commons are freely available to companies for commercial profit.

They should be regulated for fair use by all. See various discussion groups on the web • *The Natural Wealth of Nations - Harnessing the Market and the Environment* by David Roodman (governments spend over $700bn annually subsidising activities that harm the environment) • *The Politics of Money - Towards Sustainability and Economic Democracy* by Frances Hutchinson *et al*

• **Basic Needs** • Max-Neef's *matrix of needs and satisfiers* is more useful for development studies than Maslow's *hierarchy of needs.*

• **'Them' or 'Us'?** • See *An Intelligent Person's Guide to the Classics* by Peter Jones 1999 • real democracy has been very rare, perhaps only practised by Athenians from 507 to 322BC and, of religious groups, by the Quakers. It was attempted by the American Founders, particularly Thomas Jefferson. However democracy is the basis of much indigenous culture and was the basis of Gandhi's thought • Lathur is a project of ASSEFA using Gandhian techniques in Indian villages • *The Life of Mahatma Gandhi* by Louis Fischer

• **Wealth in Poverty** • see Amartya Sen's work on comparative wealth • for hunter-gatherer attitudes see *Ishmael* and *Beyond Civilization* by Daniel Quinn • *The Intimate and the Ultimate* by Vinoba Bhave, edited by Satish Kumar (dealing with land reform in India) •

• **Free Trade** • see Center for Concern factsheet on *Corporate Accountability* • Banana dispute see *Rachel's E&HW No. 679* • For policy recommendations see *Hungry for Trade* p121 • Analysis of free trade damage see *Winners and Losers, The Economist* 28 April 2001 • *Passion for Free Markets* articles by Noam Chomsky on www.zmag.org • *The Lugano Report - on*

Preserving Capitalism in the Twenty-First Century by Susan George

• **Just Change** • ACCORD at Gudalur. TN. India is also working with Oxfam • Latrine workers: see *Endless Filth* by Mari Marcel-Thekaekara.

• **WTO** • *Another World is Possible* by Fisher & Ponniah 2003 • CNES websites to "demystify the World Bank, IMF and WTO, particularly how they diminish the role of government and facilitate privatisation of service delivery often without the knowledge or consent of citizens or elected officials." • *International Trade & Sustainable Development* an Earthscan reader • *The Best Democracy Money Can Buy* by Greg Palast • *Global Spin - the Corporate Assault on Environmentalism* by Sharon Beder • *False Dawn - the Delusions of Global Capitalism* by John Gray

• **Water Denied** • many positive local books like *Rainwater Harvesting* by Shree Padre (India) • *Resource Wars* by Vandana Shiva 2002 • No lessons have been learnt and the situation is deteriorating: see New Internationalist 354 March 2003

• **The GATS** • *The Silent Takeover - Global Capitalism and the Death of Democracy* by Noreena Hertz • **Haiti**: The IMF forced Haiti to lower import tariffs on its main crop, rice; growers were driven out of business by subsidised imports from the US; Haiti fined merchants $1.4m for evading customs duty and the US witheld $30m aid in retaliation. Aristide, though democratically elected, was powerless (will the reformist President Lula of Brazil be similarly incapacitated?)

• **Ending Tyranny** • Aliance for Democracy websites to "end corporate domination, and achieve true democracy, a just society and sustainable and

equitable economy." • *The Post-Corporate World* by David C Korten 1999.
• **Civilized Values** • *What Next* by Walter Mosley • *Rogue State* by William Blum 2000 (for a fuller account of the US's disgraceful treatment of poor countries) • Pilger commentaries: http://pilger.carlton.com • *Why do People Hate America?* by Sardar and Davies 2002 • *Unholy Wars* by John K Cooley 1999 • *Perpetual Wars for Perpetual Peace* by Gore Vidal 2002.
• **The Empire** • "Full Spectrum Dominance" is the key phrase in *Joint Vision 2020* by US Department of Defense 2001 and is used as a mission statement by all branches of the US military • *The West and the Rest* by Roger Scruton 2002 • *Al Qaeda - and What it Means to be Modern* by John Gray 2003 • *Rogue Nation* by Vernon Colman
• **Imperial Tribute** • *Why are the Americans Smiling?* Hugo Salinas Price www.plata.com.mx • quote by Dr Thomas Bennett, professor at the US Naval War College, published by the US Naval Institute January 2002 pp53-56.
• **Soil** • Phosphorus a limited resource, see: Folke Gunther, *Feasta Review 2001* and www.holon.se/folke
• **Feeding the World** • see Center for Concern factsheet on *Food Security* • Royal Society quote from *Transgenic Plants and World Agriculture* July 2000 • the *Killing of the Countryside* by Graham Harvey (explores the myth of cheap food and the devastation of rural Britain by subsidies, with a few statistics that even the dimmest politician can grasp) • *From the Ground Up - Rethinking Industrial Agriculture* by Helena Norberg-Hodge *et al* • *The Great Food Gamble* by John Humphrys (a devastating indictment of what we are doing to our food and how it affects our health) • *Tending the Earth - Traditional, Sustainable Agriculture in India* by Winin Pereira • Survey of Indian Agriculture 2004 (annual) incl. Prof. MS Swaminathan • *Restoring the Earth - Visionary Solutions from the Bioneers* by Kenny Ausubel (examples of how pioneers are creating sustainable communities in the US) • *The Living Earth* by Jules Pretty (case for a shift towards a more sustainable and community-led agriculture • *Dishing up Death - Is Our Food Poisoning Us* by Jacquie Reilly (short book covering subjects like salmonella, about which Edwina Curry broke with tradition and spoke the truth) • *Fast Food Nation* by Eric Schlosser
• **Organics** • Yields: Rodale Institute in Kutztown, Pennsylvania 2001 • *Cuba: Cuba's Organic Revolution* by Walter Schwarz. Resurgence 212 • mineral content: www.foodisyourbestmedicine.com.
• **Citizens' Jury** • The Jefferson Center has prepared a short booklet describing the Citizens Jury process in detail • for official report of the procceedings in Andhra Pradesh see International Institute for Environment and Development: www.iied.org and Institute of Development Studies: www.ids.ac.uk
• **POPs & EDCs** • see also *Pandora's Poison* by J. Thornton.
• **Antibiotics** • **Vivisection**: *The Best Hope For Animals is War* by John Gray in the *New Statesman* 9.2.04. Secular reasoning argues against Christian and Humanist licence to confine, torture and kill animals that are genetically very close to *'homo sapiens'*
• **Microbes** • **Aids**: Edward Hooper, in *The River*, gives

compelling evidence that the HIV virus was transferred from chimpanzees to humans by the Wistar Institute experimenting with a polio vaccine called Chat in the Congo (Zaire) in 1957-60. The company tested Chat on more than a million Africans (though the 'patients' did not need vaccination and a polio epidemic occurred soon after in the vicinity probably caused by the vaccine). After 40 years of 'commercial confidentiality' the Royal Society was given selected samples of the vaccine to analyse and, not surprisingly, found no evidence of the HIV virus. Repeated attempts have been made by the company to establish that aids started before 1958. The US, all biotech companies and biotech scientists have an interest in denying that they could be responsible for the start of the aids epidemic since this would have devastating consequences for the lucrative biotech industry - better to blame Africans for eating bushmeat without explaining why the epidemic should happen just at this point in history (since the practice is not new) and why it should have started in that particular location. See also article by Matt Ridley in *Prospect* magazine June 2000. • see *Die Off* article on Disease.
• **Genes** • Genome destabilisation of rats: research at University of Leicester, *New Scientist* 11 May 2002 •
Genome by Matt Ridley1999 •
• **Making New Plants** • *Seeds of Doubt* by the Soil Association 2002 is based on inspections and interviews with farmers in the US and Canada. The facts have, to a great extent, been suppressed in the US by massively funded financial pressure from the biotech industry, so research from this UK organization is significant • Genetic experimentation has been carried out on the basis that most DNA is 'junk'; it is now known that this is not the case (this is an obvious probability that has been ignored in the interests of quick results) • Allergenic GM: *US NAS 2000* report on biotech foods • *The Impact of GM on Agriculture, Food and Health* by the BMA (UK) 1999 • Transfer of toxins to soil: Saxena in *NATURE* 2nd Dec 1999 • *Genetic Engineering* by Luke Anderson • The nutritional value of **GM vitamine A rice ('Golden Rice')** is a cynical PR exercise by biotech companies that is frequently quoted as the main benefit of GM crops. Indian NGOs, like SCAD in Tirunelveli, (scad@md4.vsnl.net.in) prevent vitamine A deficiency with a diet of yellow fruit and vegetables (papaya, pumpkin, etc) which grow like weeds at no cost. They say novel seeds deplete genetic diversity and make poor people dependent on bought seed. In the 350 villages advised by SCAD the problem has been eradicated simply by educating womens' groups about diet. The problem had been created by the Green Revolution and by advertising for alopathic medicines. Biotech companies know the value of yellow vegetables through their researches into patents but withold the information, presumably because it would not contribute to their profits.
• **Commercial Eugenics** • *Maybe One* by Bill McKibben 1998.
• **Commercial Eugenics** • See also the work of professor Steven Rose, Brain & Behaviour Research Group, Oxford University i.e. "The sanguine conceit that somehow we have the power to stop or direct evolution is the most arrogant fantasy of all."

Index

Glossary

C&C   Contraction and Convergence 37
DTQ   Domestic Tradable Quota 40
DU   Depleted Uranium 50
ebcu   emissions-backed currency unit 76
EDCs   endocrine-disrupting chemicals 146
EPA   US Environmental Protection Agency
EU   European Union
FTAA   Free Trade Area of the Americas 112
G8, G21, G40. Group of rich, medium, poor countries
GCI   Global Commons Institute 37
GATT   General Agreement on Tariffs and Trade
GATS   General Agreement on Trade in Services 109
GE (GM, GMO) genetic engineering
HIPCs Heavily Indebted Poor Countries 96
IMF   International Monetary Fund
IPCC   Intergovernmental Panel on Climate Change
LETS   Local Exchange Trading Schemes 77
NAFTA North American Free Trade Area
NAS   US National Academy of Sciences
NIBC   Nano-Bio-Info-Cogno 173

PNAC   Project for the New American Century 125
POPs   persistant organic pollutants 146
SERs   Special Emission Rights 76
TRIPS Trade Related Intellectual Property Rights 108
UNDP   United Nations Development Program
USDA   US Department of Agriculture
WTO   World Trade Organization 10